Revolution From Within

Co-operatives and co-operation in British industry

Michael Young and
Marianne Rigge

Weidenfeld and Nicolson   London

Printed in Great Britain by
Butler & Tanner Ltd, Frome and London

evolution From Within

L

Contents

Introduction The need for a third sector vii
Chapter 1 Inner cities and outer islands 1
Chapter 2 Why the renewal? 13
Chapter 3 What is a worker co-operative? 42
Chapter 4 Ways of getting started 61
Chapter 5 Co-operation between co-operatives 79
Chapter 6 The role of the state 104
Chapter 7 The new mechanized peasantry 129
Appendix Checkpoints for would-be
co-operators 152

References 171
Further reading 176
Index 181

Introduction
The need for a third sector

The third sector cannot be defined without reference to the other two. The implied contrast is on the one hand with the first sector of the economy, the private enterprise one in which the means of production are owned by capitalists, and on the other with the second sector, the state sector in which the means of production are owned by the state. In the third sector, the common owner-ship sector, the means of production are owned neither by capitalists nor by the state but by a partnership of consumers or workers.

Consumer ownership has been the best-known so far, taking the form of consumer co-operatives in wholesaling and retailing, of housing co-operatives and also of building societies and mu-tual insurance offices which have flourished so exceedingly in this century although unfortunately not with any pride in their co-operative ancestry. Farmers, horticulturists and fishermen, as independent producers, also own their special-purpose co-oper-atives. Our main interest in this book, however, is with worker ownership. It cannot be called ownership by employees because in such concerns there is no employer – it is self-employment as it is self-management but on a collective rather than an indivi-dual scale. For the moment we shall describe this kind of co-operative as a business which is owned and controlled by those who work in it, leaving a fuller definition until later. The issue we shall be exploring in this book is how far such businesses could have a much larger part to play in the future in what could then be an even more substantial third sector. Worker co-oper-atives have already expanded rapidly in the last decade and especially since the onset of the recession. There are five new ones every week.

One reason for the interest is the bitterness that exists in industry at present, with the workers on one side engaged in a more or less continual battle with the employers on the other. This industrial civil war has been worse in Britain than elsewhere and has, over the last decade, helped to make our inflation worse than elsewhere. There would be little point in co-operatives unless they fostered better human relations, especially between managers and workers. Co-operation is *about* human relations.

On the shop floor or in the shop the actual relationships which do not run smoothly are not so much between owners and employees as between managers and employees, even though capitalist businesses are commonly thought of as being 'owned' by their private shareholders, and nationalized businesses by the state. But in both the concept of ownership has largely been drained of its meaning. Ownership is nothing (or nothing much) without control. But in large companies it is not the shareholders who exercise control but the managers, who are either members of a self-perpetuating board of directors or appointed by that board.

It is not, of course, quite the same with the state. As the sole owner of a nationalized industry like coal or steel or a public service like the National Health Service the state is in a more powerful position than large numbers of private shareholders can ever be. If it can mobilize its own power it can exert control. But the weakness of the state as an owner of business is that it has no gender. It is neither male nor female; it is neuter. It is an it, which in this case means it is made up of thousands of individual people – not just Ministers, but MPs, civil servants and officials of every conceivable kind and degree jostling for power with each other. Being such a great jellyfish, it can seldom collect itself together sufficiently to exercise anything more than the most general control of the other it, the state businesses, which it nominally owns. As in capitalist businesses, control therefore also rests with managers organized into bureaucracies of much the same kind.

Managers have all the more power because nominally they are responsible to someone else, shareholders or state, for the way in which it is exercised. It can be uncomfortable to have power over other people which is in a sense naked power, derived solely from the office the manager has in the organization. It is more acceptable to clothe the power with legitimacy by making it nominally conditional, exercised not on behalf of themselves but on behalf of someone else, in this case the shareholder or the state. A manager who sacks people or is offensive to them in other ways can say he is doing it not so much for his own sake as for someone else's. But his allegiance to this outside party is more sham than genuine.

If the pretence has some positive psychological value for the manager in giving him confidence it has only negative value for employees who are liable to give it much more credibility than it deserves. They still think in terms of the capitalist rather than the managerial system of business. 'The management' always seems to be acting on behalf of absentee shareholders or a remote state who grasp for profits or other advantages which seldom coincide with the things that employees want out of the business. The two sides – management and employees – are maintained as separate, conflicting entities by the system that encourages managers to consider themselves the agents of a third party in whose name they can rule as permanent regents.

As a counter to this the revolutionary idea behind the co-operative is that the two sides should be merged by removing the private and state shareholders from the scene and making the managers responsible to the workers. This would restore some meaning to ownership.

At its best, ownership implies responsibility. The owner of a house, say, is responsible for its upkeep. If all the workers including the managers owned their businesses they would share a sense of common responsibility for them. There could be unity in place of the disunity that prevails at present.

Outside shareholders in large companies have so little power in the ordinary way that managerial accountability is largely a fiction. Inside shareholders – where that is what workers become – could be another matter altogether. They would have a special interest in their business and in the way it is managed. They could be effective as owners because they would be on the spot, like members of family businesses who both own and work in them.

Not that it could happen all at once. If the state suddenly

compelled all companies and public services to be made into co-operatives it would certainly be inviting disaster. People need to be persuaded to 'co-operate', as managers or worker-owners, not forced by law to do so.

Needless to say, changes in the patterns of ownership will only have the effect we hope for if they are accompanied by changes in the attitudes of both trade unions and management. As it happens, the two of them have traditionally been associated with the two traditional political parties, and each of these in turn with the first or the second sectors of the economy. Co-operation has not been dear to either of them. So it would be especially fitting for a new approach to the old problems of industrial relations to come from the new political party, the SDP, and its partner in the Alliance. The SDP can make the cause of co-operatives its own and has indeed already expressed its strong support for them.[1] The third sector and the third party could go together. Not that the third party would want to claim any monopoly of interest. The more there is on the part of the other parties as well, the better the chances for a rapid development.

In Chapter 1 we present some examples to give an impression of what worker co-operatives are like, and then move on to account for their revival in Chapter 2 and to mention the two great problems identified by Beatrice Webb nearly a century ago and which still exist. We describe the main types of co-operative in Chapter 3, look at the ways in which co-ops start in Chapter 4, propose how co-operatives could co-operate together more effectively in Chapter 5, outline the help that could be given by the state in Chapter 6, and in Chapter 7 consider the wider question of whether or not the march of technology will make work less boring and hence more rewarding for workers to take an interest in, instead of gladly leaving responsibility to others, as they so often do at present.

We would like to acknowledge the great help we have had from many people, including particularly D.G. Bailey, Elise Bailey, John Berry, R. Bluer, Chris Brooks, Stephen Cadney, Cairns Campbell, Mike Campbell, Peter Clarke, Chris Cornforth, Stephen Crabtree, Paul Derrick, George Goyder, Mark Goyder,

Denis Gregory, Branko Horvat, George Jones, Lord Kennet, Dennis Lawrence, Chris Logan, Gerda Lowen, Richard Macfarlane, Laura McGillivray, Iain MacInnes, Colin E. McKone, Father J.A. Macmillan, Jimmy Marshall, Dr R.L. Marshall, John Morley (EEC), John Morley (Plunkett Foundation), Robert Oakeshott, Hans Ollman, Lord Oram, Edgar Parnell, Andrew Phillips, J.A. Powell, David Ralley, J.S. Sadler, Lord Seebohm, N.F. Shatford, Peter Smith, Robert Smith, Leonora Stettner, R.J. Storey, Ian Swinney, Alan Taylor, Peter Walker, Jennifer Wates, W.P. Watkins, Sir Frederick Wood, and Ralph Woolf. Our special thanks also to Sue Chisholm, Jessica Gould and Wyn Tucker who did so much to help in the preparation of the various drafts of this book.

1   Inner cities and outer islands

To begin with, the manager was ill-at-ease behind his desk. He did not look as if his powerful frame was meant to be covered by a suit. But his eyes lit up as he told us how delighted the shop stewards were by the profits the co-operative was making. The musicians in their evening dress waiting for the conductor to make his entrance into the Festival Hall knew that the conductor had not hired them: an orchestral co-operative, they had hired him. The girl in her flowered shirt and jeans was very serious when she said she looked forward to getting her licence to drive a heavy goods vehicle; she would be more useful to her co-operative then. The priest in his fisherman's sweater was also a ferryman who would take any members of the co-operative (or anyone else) across the water not to Hades but to his promised land.

They all showed that unless their distinguishing mark was that they shared a certain enthusiasm, they, and their co-operatives, are as diverse as can be.

Most worker co-operatives are of recent origin. They are at present doubling their number every two years. But as a reminder that some are far from new we visited Avalon Footwear at Rothwell, near Kettering. It was started in 1892 by a band of working-class people who were determined to prove that they as workers could manage industry just as well as their former bosses. The founders have been proved right. The co-operative has continued, as it began, to make good-quality welted and cemented men's shoes in two different factories, one up the hill which appropriately enough makes the uppers and another at the bottom which makes the bottoms. About half of the 120 members are men and half women – the cutting, or 'clicking', as it is known in the trade, is a man's job along with the assembling and finishing, while the stitching, cleaning and boxing are women's jobs. Everyone, man or woman, is a member of the trade union, whose role is the traditional one, protecting the interests of its members against the committee of management. Although this committee, which appoints the general manager, is elected by all the members, they consider the union is as necessary, or almost as necessary, as in a capitalist company. So far the formula has worked. Setback though the recession has been, Avalon has managed to weather it, partly because it has continued to get orders from within the co-operative movement, from the Co-operative Wholesale Society and Co-operative Retail Services. There have been no redundancies.

Another co-operative was like Avalon in being started by working-class people, but in very different circumstances. Avalon was started from scratch whereas the Inchinnan factory in Glasgow had belonged to the Dunlop company before it was closed down in the autumn of 1981. The building is still there, as huge as when it was a thriving works employing 5,000 people – span after span stretches away into the far distance – but now it is empty, like a derelict ship waiting to be broken up. The only place where there are still people is slightly to one side, in a smaller self-contained building. There the new co-op has its headquarters, in fact its only quarters.

To get them going, co-operatives often depend just as much as any other kind of business upon an enterprising individual. Here he was Jimmy Marshall, a young, tough Clydesider who was convenor of shop stewards for the Amalgamated Union of Engineering Workers. He was not prepared to sit back and let his own and his members' jobs disappear, not at any rate without making a fight of it. The union's first effort went into trying to persuade Dunlop to keep in being the machine shop in which the engineers worked, repairing and making the moulds which press tyres into shape. The management refused, then to the surprise of the workers counter-suggested that they should keep the business going themselves, as a co-operative. 'Co-operative?', said Jimmy Marshall, 'what is that?', illustrating how little known the notion still is in industry.

Jimmy Marshall and his fellow shop-stewards set about finding out what was meant. Someone in Liverpool told them about the Scottish Co-operatives Development Committee (described in Chapter 5) which again they had never heard of although its office was close by in their own city of Glasgow. The people there were just what they needed to help them. They knew how to establish a co-operative; they also knew how to prepare a plan for the business and assess its prospects. After looking into it, they decided that the workers might make a go of it, on two conditions. The first was that every worker should become a member of the co-operative and invest in it £1,000 of his own money as loan capital, finding the money in one lump out of redundancy payments or, if they could not do that because they had not been employed by Dunlop long enough to entitle them to so much, building it up week by week by deduction from their wages. The capital they put together to start with from their own money was £48,000. Once they showed they were confident enough to put their money at risk in this way, the second condition could be more easily met, which was that Dunlop would help to breathe life into the phoenix. Sir Campbell Fraser, Dunlop's Scottish Chairman, now President of the CBI for the United Kingdom as a whole, proved a powerful ally. The company agreed to guarantee enough work for at least fifteen engineers in the machine shop, which they could add to by getting contracts from wherever they could find them; to let the co-op have the premises rent-free for its first six months; and to lease the electronic borers and other machines at a low charge until the co-op could afford to buy them.

So far the new enterprise has been successful, with three chief benefits flowing from being a co-op. The first was that everyone put his back into the job as he had never done before. They were no longer working for an employer whom they always felt (at least until the last few months when Dunlop had been so unexpectedly generous) was ripping them off; they were working for themselves, and behaved as though they were. All members met once a fortnight during the lunch break to take their own decisions. At one of these meetings they decided to do away with clocking in. Time-keeping was so good that the clock was no longer needed. The second benefit was that they became very much more flexible about who should do what. They abolished the customary demarcations between one job and another on whose sanctity their union, and they themselves, had always been so insistent. In the new circumstances anyone was prepared to do anyone else's job if need be. Fitters did turning, turners grinding, after whatever additional training was necessary. The third was that in Jimmy Marshall they had a manager they could trust, manager being what he became at least for the time being; and likewise the two other directors of the co-op who had both been shop stewards. Inchinnan was a 'trade union co-op' which enjoyed the fullest support from local AUEW officials. It is still a 100 per cent union shop. The manager was paid the same as other skilled men in the AUEW but less than the foreman and draughtsman.

All this showed in increased efficiency. For each contract they got from Dunlop, the Avon tyre company or anyone else they had to put in a tender. These were generally lower than their competitors' – for moulds for Avon the co-op quoted £888 as against the competitive quote of £1,500. The co-op also produced the goods faster – for deliveries of some particular segments of moulds one firm quoted 12–15 weeks delivery, the co-op three weeks. While they were keeping up their old business they were also looking for new markets, there being an obvious need to reduce their dependence on the tyre industry and on Dunlop in particular. The co-op appointed a firm of consultants to do market research for them to help find new customers, preferably having nothing at all to do with tyres. One possibility being looked into was the manufacture of pressure bottles for North Sea gas for selling to farmers.

The London Philharmonic Orchestra is about as different from Avalon and Inchinnan as it could be, middle-class in its composition and far removed from manufacturing. It is one of a number of orchestras which have become co-operatives, stemming from the decision in 1905 by the players of the London Symphony Orchestra to 'form something akin to a Musical Republic'.[2] The right and obligation to buy shares in the company was limited to 'performing members of the LSO'. The Royal Philharmonic Orchestra followed suit in 1963 and the Philharmonia later. Orchestras are particularly suitable for co-operatives in one way: they need very little capital, all the more so because the members provide their own instruments.

The specific prompt for the LPO was not a closure as at Inchinnan but the departure of the 'boss'. Shortly after the outbreak of the Second World War, Sir Thomas Beecham, the orchestra's founder and its famous conductor, left England for the USA. There was no one to take his place. If the orchestra was to keep going at all it had to be by the efforts of its own players. When eventually Beecham returned from America his former orchestra was his no longer, nor any other conductor's. Any conductor from anywhere in the world knows that in the LPO it is the players who are in command: the maestro may be able to behave like one in Berlin or Vienna, New York or Chicago. Here he has not only to be a highly proficient musician; he also has to mind his manners if he wants to be commissioned again, and the same goes for soloists.

Each playing member of the orchestra – seventy-six of them in March 1982 – has one £1 share and one vote to go with it. They elect the eight-man board of directors annually, all of whom except for the managing director, Stephen Crabtree, have to be playing members themselves. Board membership rotates. Being on it means extra work and few players are eager for that on top of their already arduous life – hence the rotation. The board has total artistic and financial responsibility for everything that the orchestra does.

One reason why membership of the board is no sinecure is that it appoints all new players. There are always plenty of people wanting to join. Their names are stockpiled until there is a vacancy. If they are looking for a new violinist they may audition thirty, each of whom has to play to the entire board together with any other member of the co-operative who wishes to listen. We do not know of any other co-op of such a size where the whole board decides who shall be admitted; nor of any other where the qualifications required are so absolute. An orchestra is a metaphor for a co-operative of any kind as well as in this case being an actual one. No co-operative of any kind will work unless the parts its members play are 'orchestrated' just as any will fail if (to continue with musical metaphors) its members are out of tune, not in key, not in unison, prima donna-ish.

Despite all the trouble that is taken, mistakes are sometimes made. The best players can go off form or put less effort into rehearsing. If that happens any member not satisfied with the musicianship of another, whether or not in the same section of the orchestra, can report the player to the board. If the player is a board member he has to leave the room while the quality of his playing is discussed. Whoever he is, he may be asked to go through an audition again. Any player whose competence has been questioned has a right to be told just what has been said about him or her. The players support as well as criticize each other. When one of them contracted multiple sclerosis all the others rallied round and gave both moral and financial help. An outside supporter of the orchestra paid for specal railings to be put up in concert halls so that he could continue to play.

In one way the orchestra is like Avalon and Inchinnan. It is a closed shop: every player must be a member of the Musicians' Union. There is no problem about ordinary wages as the LPO pays slightly more than union rates, but sometimes there is when the orchestra is doing a recording and cannot, according to the union, record for more than twenty minutes in a three-hour recording session. The union does not stop people swapping roles. At an industrial tribunal to which a member appealed against his dismissal another of the players was put on the witness stand and asked what his job was. He said he was a cellist. 'Do you hold any other position?' 'Yes, I'm a director.' 'Anything else?' 'Yes, I'm a union steward.'

It is not an easy life. From the Arts Council they get a subsidy which is tiny compared to most of the large orchestras of the world. The Berlin Philharmonic, for instance, gets 93 per cent of its costs covered by a subsidy from the government, and the percentage is of a much larger total. Lacking that kind of aid, the co-op members have to work extremely hard. If they are offered three sessions a day for a week they have to accept even if the day sessions are followed by evening concerts as well, and the work is tougher still on tours of the USA, China or Europe. A player who wants even one day off in the year has to ask a special Release Committee. Holidays are ruled out in the summer, when the LPO is the resident orchestra at Glyndebourne, and it always appears at the Edinburgh Festival. Overwork poses a constant threat to standards. So far they have never been allowed to fall. The LPO is still one of the world's great orchestras.

SUMA in Leeds is different again. Unlike the three previous co-operatives it belongs to the alternative movement, as it is called. For that its business as a wholefood wholesaler fits perfectly. Although a comparatively new co-op it is in an old tradition. In 1844 the initiators of the first co-operative shop at Rochdale on the other side of the Pennines were proud to sell pure food, unlike the mill-owners who made a profit out of selling shoddy goods and adulterated foodstuffs in their factory shops. SUMA goes further, with nuts and brown sugar, sunflower oil and muesli, dried fruit, green pasta and wholemeal flour. They are 'pure' in a way that ordinary commercially produced, commercially advertised and commercially sold foods are not. Wholefoods have become a symbol for the alternative movement, just as co-ops themselves have done. In this trade a co-op is doubly qualified.

Whereas in the other three places the pay is the rate for the job, with differentials much the same as in other companies in their line of business, the members of SUMA believe in equal wages. All workers get the same take-home pay but with additions for people with special needs. One woman was paid £5 a week extra because she had children to look after. A man with three children was allowed extra money as well. More unusual still is the absence of any manager. The members do not believe there should be one. Responsibility is delegated to several different people for decisions in different parts of the enterprise, each being accountable to the general meeting of all the members which is held once a week. They all recognize that decisions cannot be collective unless each member passes on to the others any relevant information that he or she has. They also recognize that they could not persist with this form of direct rather than representative democracy if the co-op became much larger than it is. Seventeen full-time members, one full-time probationer, one temporary full-timer and four regular part-timers were employed at the time this book was sent to the press.

Much of the work is driving, from SUMA's warehouse in Leeds to London or elsewhere to collect supplies or from Leeds to any of the 140 or so wholefood shops in the north of England, many of which belong to the Federation of Northern Wholefood Co-ops. Local deliveries are made by one of the co-op's three vans; most take turns with that and drive for one day a week. The 32-ton lorry is another matter. The law requires its drivers to have a heavy goods vehicle licence. People have to train rigorously for it; it costs £300 to take the test and after that at least three months' solid driving are needed to gain proficiency.

By ordinary business standards, or by those of the other three co-ops mentioned so far, the management structure or rather relative lack of it, is unusual. It has also been successful. Turnover and profits have grown each year. Turnover in the current year will be about £2 million, and profits enough to finance large capital expenditure. A good deal of financial and practical support is given to other co-ops from SUMA's loan fund.

The fifth example is not of a worker co-operative at all but of a new affair, a community co-operative which is a kind of hybrid between a worker and consumer co-op but without the constitution of either. Near-co-operative businesses abound on all sides, having their own structures and being built around a common bond which unites the people who *are* the organization. In the case of community co-operatives the common bond is not so much the one which ties together the members of the other co-ops we have described – working together in order to make a living – as living together in order to create work.

This community co-operative is on the rocky, treeless island of Eriskay in the Outer Hebrides. It dates from 1979 when Rena MacKinnon, the widow of a leading island figure, heard a talk about the new Co-Chomunns (as community co-ops are called in Gaelic) on the neighbouring island of South Uist. There she heard that the Highlands and Islands Development Board – a government agency – was prepared to help with money and advice if local people took the initiative. The deal was that the Board would up to an agreed figure match £1 for £1 the money put up by local people and that their field officer, Coinneach Maclean, would help them all along the way.

Many of those Mrs MacKinnon talked to at first were extremely sceptical – how could they possibly make a success of something which had defeated others before? Ordinary people run a shop? In as remote a place as this? The most telling fact on her side was that people had to go to South Uist for their shopping. The islanders grow their own potatoes and other vegetables in ridges made of topsoil painfully spooned off the rock. Some of them have hardy chickens. They can get as much free fish as they like from one of the six trawlers which are, along with the lobster creels, the mainstay of the economy. But for ordinary groceries the islanders were then at a serious disadvantage.

The ferry cost £2 and the taxi to take them to the shop and back £8. Since they bought as much as they could carry to cut down on the costs of the journey, the shopping was always in danger of being soaked by salt water, especially if the seas had risen while they were away. Their goods could also be knocked about on board the ferry, or when being manhandled off the boat, until, finally, they were lugged up the steep road which led from the quay to their homes.

The islanders were eventually persuaded. Virtually every family put up their share of the Co-Chomunn's capital which was promptly matched by the Board. All they then needed was a manager whose salary would also be paid by the Board – 100 per cent in the first year, 50 per cent for the next two. Nineteen people replied to the advertisement. For the last of the candidates put on the shortlist, Iain MacInnes, they had to wait. He was employed on an oil rig in the North Sea and so was a week late for the interview. He was not at all put off by the bareness of the island, its rocks breaking out like boils from the thin topsoil, its lack of trees, its high winds. He knew it well, was indeed almost a native. Although he was born in Glasgow, his father was from Eriskay; for as far back in his life as he could remember he had come there for his holidays to stay with one or other of his many relatives. He continued to do so while he was studying chemistry at Strathclyde University and when he was working as a labourer and in many jobs afterwards. A stocky, smiling, easy-going man, his personality, his range of experience, his local contacts and his understanding of Gaelic gave him the edge over the others. He got the job.

In due course the shop was opened in a newly designed building filled with groceries, later to be joined by whisky and beer. With help from the Board, the Co-operative Wholesale Society was persuaded to deliver container loads to the quay on the other side of the water, without adding anything on for transport costs. Mr MacInnes even manages to sell bread at the same price as in Inverness where it is baked – though it has to be driven to Kyle of Lochalsh, ferried to Skye, driven through Skye to Uig, ferried to Lochmaddy and then through North and South Uist to Eriskay. The shop has a sub-post office and an off-licence.

Once the shop was running and giving jobs to its staff of two women, later expanded to three, Iain MacInnes was able to turn his attention to the fishermen's co-op. This already existed without being very active. He has brought it to life, above all by installing a large diesel tank and buying oil and other chandlery supplies for it through an all-Scotland fishing co-op. Once again, the bulk prices are no higher than anywhere else. Indeed, the trawlers can now get their fuel more cheaply on Eriskay than they can from commercial dealers at Mallaig where they land their catches of white fish and prawns. Any fuel profits are shared equally between the fishing co-operative and the community co-operative.

One cottage industry giving local employment which has been helped is hand-knitting. The Eriskay jersey was designed for fishermen, close-fitting and knitted in the round, without seams and with traditional motifs knitted in, such as the starfish, the harbour steps, the anchor, the fish-net and the wave. Over the generations mothers have handed the skill down to their daughters. Now the co-operative has begun to find a wider market for the jerseys and employs eleven women part-time to make them.

A start has also been made on an oyster farm, sited in an unusual place. In 1941 a good ship with a strange name, the *Politician*, foundered on the rocks of Eriskay with a cargo of 20,000 cases of whisky on board. There was no *Whisky Galore* for the islanders, although not all remained under the water until the excisemen rushed over from the mainland to blow it up. Fortunately, they did not completely destroy the ship. Today, the wreck is the underwater base for yet another budding off-shoot which will grow Japanese oysters.

Further expansion is being planned. Two derelict cottages have been bought for conversion into self-catering holiday lets for fish- and fishing-lovers and for Eriskay emigrants in Canada,

Australia or the USA who want to see their old home. There is another plan for breaking in some of the wild grey Eriskay ponies, half-way between a Shetland and a horse, and hiring them to the holiday-makers for pony-trekking; another for processing fish and selling it on South Uist; another for growing early vegetables under polythene; another for a slipway so that trawlers can be repaired on the spot more easily than at present; and still another for a new community hall. Before the Co-Chomunn few thought the community could get together for any common purpose like building a new hall. When we visited the island people were confident they could raise amongst themselves the £17,000 they needed as their contribution to its cost.

Mr MacInnes is one key figure in the Co-Chomunn and another is Father MacMillan, the island's young Gaelic-speaking Catholic priest. To raise money for the hall he played the bagpipes while water-skiing, with sponsors for every quarter-mile he stayed upright. Known to everyone as Father Johnarchie from his first names, with the accent on the second syllable, he is both secretary and treasurer of the co-op as well as one of its main voluntary helpers. He takes parties of children in the co-op's minibus to the mainland on the new vehicle ferry, or goes to Glasgow for special collections of goods the cws cannot deliver; he drives the tractor over with a party of other strong men to load the container of groceries; he sometimes repairs the engines of the fishing boats and he is always ready to act as an extra ferryman in his own speedboat when the ordinary one is not running. The islanders crowd into his church for Mass every Sunday.

The third key figure in the Co-Chomunn has been Ronald Campbell, its chairman until recently. He told us, as everyone else did, that without the support of the HIDB they never would have got going. So much has been happening since they did that he can hardly keep up with it all. 'I think', he said to us, 'that next year I ought to give someone else a chance to be Chairman, especially if it is someone who can give more time to it. I'm away fishing for many days a week.'

The Cho-Chomunn is one of the reasons why life has got better. After a century's emigration the population stabilized in the 1960s and since then has grown, with the number of children rising now that fewer young men and women leave. Unemployment on the mainland is a powerful deterrent. On Eriskay only three men have registered as unemployed. Eriskay is on the up-and-up whereas to the islanders Britain as a whole is on the down-and-down.

If competition takes many forms, so evidently does co-operation. The motive in Kettering nearly a century ago was the wish of a group of workers to set up on their own within the co-operative movement; in Glasgow the need to preserve some jobs about to be lost in one of the factory closures which have become so depressingly common in recent years; in London the wish to keep a great orchestra in being; in Leeds the hope of creating more than just a new way of working; in Eriskay to give a small remote community a few advantages of the large. Between them they may, before we begin to treat our subject more generally, serve to emphasize the fact that every one of the co-operatives we shall be talking about in the chapters to come is also unique.

2   Why the renewal?

Ideas can never be buried like people. Dust to dust will not return. But ideas, however dead they seem and however deeply buried, are liable to work their way out when their time comes again and gain a kind of immortality above ground as though they had never been put away below it.

We doubt whether any members of the co-operatives described in the last chapter would call themselves Owenites and few even recognize the term which was common parlance for a good many years after the death of Robert Owen himself. His name lived on for a time because he had once been one of the most influential men in Britain and also in Europe and in the USA where he addressed the President and the full Congress. He was famous for demonstrating in the cotton mill he acquired at New Lanark in 1799 that a manager could be a humanitarian *and* make a great deal of money. He was still more famous for speaking so much out of character for a cotton master in the early days of the Industrial Revolution. He told everyone that a co-operative system in industry in which one man's gain would not be another man's loss[3] would be on all counts superior to the competitive system from which he, as a businessman, had gained so much. A co-operative community would, he thought, encourage the right kind of character formation and create people who wanted to work for the good of others as well as themselves. To deal with heavy unemployment after the defeat of Napoleon in 1815 he advocated 'villages of co-operation' which parishes and the state would put money into instead of giving doles or relief to keep people in idleness. In these villages, as at New Lanark, people would be able to find work in a setting where they did not have to be in conflict with each other to make a living. He was not the inventor of co-operatives – there had been many co-operative corn mills in the eighteenth century, a Weavers' Society at Fenwick in Ayrshire and many Victualling Societies – but he became their inspiration.

'Owenism' had great appeal for people flung about by the turbulence of the Industrial Revolution and without any comfort from a ruling class which was only too content to believe with Burke that it was not 'within the competence of the government, taken as a government, or even the rich, as rich, to supply to the poor those necessaries which it has pleased the Divine Providence for awhile to withhold from them'.[4] If necessaries *were* supplied they were often enough adulterated.[5] In reaction people were only too glad to follow Owen into the Grand National Consolidated Trades Union which had over half a million members early in 1834, and into the Grand National Moral Union of the Productive Classes; their hope, like his, being that they could create a new moral order which would make all intelligent, charitable and kind to each other.

The two Grand Nationals were short-lived. Owen lost his pre-eminence. Co-operation as the foundation of a new moral order was, as the Victorian Age settled into its heyday, overlaid by a characteristic individualism based on another view of human potential. According to the Benthamite utilitarians who gained such an intellectual ascendancy, people were motivated by self-interest almost alone, being bound by their personal imperatives to maximize pleasure and minimize pain. The economists who held to the same basic doctrine regarded these same self-interested individuals not as villains but as heroes of the market, the prompters of all economic activity. They were in the social sphere followers of Darwin and they saw in the doctrine of natural selection an affirmation of the primacy of competition and conflict throughout the whole evolutionary process.

The opposite view was never lost from sight: it had also to be recognized that man is a social animal and achieves almost all the success he has in groups, that is, in co-operation with others with as much need to work and live together as he has. But this propensity, to co-operate, was for long subordinated, in the way people thought about the means of achieving the good society, to the opposite propensity, to compete. The circle was squared by asserting that competition would, as it worked out in practice, secure the same ends as co-operation, thus providing the necessary moral underpinning for capitalism ever since and incidentally illustrating the rule that the more ruthlessness people have the more important it is to them to assert their own lack of it. As Tawney put it, Adam Smith and his successors did a great service by converting a 'natural frailty into a resounding virtue'.[6] Merely by following their own self-interest people would, through the operation of the 'invisible hand', automatically secure the greatest good not just of themselves but of the greatest number in society. Have ever men out for themselves been so comforted as by the Smith doctrine that they are really benefactors after all: that if only they compete with each other for profit they will be led to promote an end – in the public welfare – which did not even need to be part of their immediate intention?

The doctrine, dressed up in new colours though it has been again and again, most recently by the Thatcher Government, has always had one weak point. It appeals more to the minority of victors than to the majority of those vanquished in the general competition. To the downtrodden of the last century Owen remained more of a guiding light than Bentham or Adam Smith; and some of them continued to follow Owen not so much by elaborating his ideology of co-operation as by showing to better effect than in the previous century how it could be worked out in practice. The most famous of them have gone down in history as the Rochdale Pioneers. They rejected the invisible hand. They preferred to work with their own real hands to build something of value to the members of their community. They believed that men would best serve the general interest when they tried to do so directly, through mutual aid, and that self-government was the best form of government as much in commerce as in politics; the humble instrument to their purpose was a shop in Toad Lane, in Rochdale. It opened its doors in 1844, the same year in the 'Hungry Forties' in which Friedrich Engels published his scarifying report on industrial Lancashire. After referring to the continual prosecutions of traders for selling tainted or poisonous goods, Engels gave a picture of the age in terms of its food.

The habitual food of the individual working man naturally varies according to his wages. The better paid workers, especially those in whose families every member is able to earn something, have good food as long as this state of things lasts; meat daily, and bacon and cheese for supper. Where wages are less, meat is used only two or three times a week, and the proportion of bread and potatoes increases. Descending gradually, we find the animal food reduced to a small piece of bacon cut up with the potatoes; lower still, even this disappears, and there remain only bread, cheese, porridge, and potatoes, until on the lowest round of the ladder, among the Irish, potates form the sole food. As an accompaniment weak tea, with perhaps a little sugar, milk, or spirits, is universally drunk ... But all this pre-supposes that the workman has work. When he has none he is wholly at the mercy of accident, and eats what is given him, what he can beg or steal. And, if he gets nothing, he simply starves, as we have seen.[7]

The Pioneers belonged to a larger protest against an urban society which had torn people out of a traditional way of life. If harsh in the extreme for most of those who did not own land, rural life had at least furnished to the individual some rudiment of communal support. The men and women of Rochdale wanted to do the same. They believed that by pooling their purchasing power they could provide better goods, for themselves of course – self-interest was always present and acknowledged – and for others as well and could also accumulate a capital fund sufficient to finance their own self-employment. They planned to give better value at lower prices than those supplied by their own employer (who often tried, as we said before, to insist that they should buy adulterated food and shoddy goods at his factory shop) or by small traders. The common practice of ordinary shopkeepers at that time was to lend money to their customers at high interest rates in return for an undertaking to buy everything from them, whatever the quality of it or whatever the price. The co-operators showed that they could relieve themselves and others from this imposition.

They were pioneers not just of a new form of business. At that time neither working men nor working women had the vote in national or local elections. They were largely excluded from the polity. They had no soundly-based trade unions to protect them. They had little or no education with which to challenge those who had education, wealth and power. In the words of an outstanding book on the subject, in these circumstances they 'set out to create for themselves citizenship of a society within society'.⁸ This they did by throwing membership of their co-operatives open to anyone and, since this was what citizenship implied, arranging for their government on the same principle of one member, one vote that they believed should operate in the political domain of the country. Once profit could no longer accrue to an individual, labour was no longer the servant of capital. Part of any surplus – a term co-operators prefer to 'profit' – had always to be devoted to education.

The founders of a shop were looking beyond its counters; they hoped to demonstrate the possibility of a more civilized life for working people, and not just by establishing a temperance hotel, one of their objects which luckily they did not succeed in achieving. A comment in one of the many co-operative journals of the last century shows how uplifting an occasion it was when co-operation extended itself in 1888 into another working-class area, Bow and Bromley in East London.

> On Friday, the 22nd of March, at two p.m., the doors of the new store, or rather the two new stores, were thrown open, and members and non-members flocked in to make their trial purchases. Our friends at Bow and Bromley are to be heartily congratulated on getting their store so soon, and also on their good fortune in recognising that they have only taken the first step, and that the best and hardest and most persistent work remains to be done. It is so easy to gauge the success of co-operation by the financial prosperity of the store; to forget that its significance lies in its being the visible sign of a closer bond between men, an outpost, as it were, of a general forward movement towards the establishment of a commonwealth founded not on increased facilities for feeding and being clothed as the store offers, but on a system of labour organised by workers, built up by the growth of character and social virtue amongst the people, and steadfastly governed by the idea of a fuller and nobler life for all men.⁹

Before long the Society would be buying a horse and cart for deliveries to its members.

The co-operative societies in Bow and Bromley, as elsewhere, belonged to, as well as encouraged, a still larger Victorian movement of mutual friendly societies and mutual insurance offices which provided some security for their members long before the Welfare State had been thought of; mechanics'and artisans' institutes where people who had little formal schooling continued their education on their own initiative; and local building societies in places like Halifax made up of hundreds of thousands of working people who also wanted to build or buy their own houses and which have in the course of time become mighty bureacracies very far removed from the shop in Toad Lane. These all flourished well enough, as did the co-operative retail societies in direct line of descent from Rochdale. By 1920 these societies had enrolled as members three out of every seven families in Britain and supplied them with half their food and one tenth of their other household possessions.[10]

Producer co-operatives which were owned by the workers in them also grew in number. Indeed, for many years after 1844 it was an open question whether the movement would 'go producer' or 'go consumer'. Producer co-operatives, after a great expansion up to the 1860s and then a great decline in the same decade, put on a spurt in the last three decades of the century – from 15 in 1874 to 109 in 1905 – and in a different form, that of Guild Socialism, came to great prominence after the First World War. The Guild Socialists wanted the state to take over this or that industry and, having brought it into public ownership, eschew state socialism and give responsibility for its management to the trade unions.[11] Wage rates would then be settled in consultation between representatives of producers and consumers. The Government would have none of it. The miners and railwaymen who at that time favoured such a system, and the postal workers likewise, were ignored. To make some progress the guildsmen had to do what they could within the capitalist system. This they did most notably by establishing the National Building Guild. In 1921 and 1922 this was operating throughout the country on a large scale. But the slump of the period eventually killed it off and Guild Socialism lived on only as an idea, if a powerful one. The co-operative movement went consumer until the retail societies began to shrink in the middle years of the present century.

This shrinkage is not due to a disappearance of people's co-operativeness or, to put it another way, their sense of fraternity.

The explanation is more that their energies were diverted from co-operative societies and the like into the creation of what in the course of time became the predominant working-class institution. Trade unions appeared in some strength after co-ops were formed, and it took many decades of bitter struggle before they won full recognition from the law and from employers. This they only did to the full when the political party they helped to form – their working-class party, the Labour Party – had ousted the Liberals from their position as the pre-eminent party of reform. It looked until recently as though they had done this with such success that on the left of British politics Labour would remain unchallengeable.

As much as co-operatives, unions have relied for their sinew on human solidarity rather than individual competitiveness. The virtue they appeal to has been the willingness of people to co-operate for the common good or at least for that of the sectional group to which they belong. Unless we stand together we shall fall together. How many times has that been said? – particularly when unionists have been called out on strike and been asked to sacrifice their earnings for the sake of the collective, and of course for the sake of each one of them as well. If it has been all for each it has also been each for all.

The movement would not have grown as it has done unless there had been a great deal to co-operate *against*. The trade unions have traditionally been anti-capitalist, not on some general ground of principle, although that has come into it as well, but because capitalism in the manner in which it has operated in the workplace has borne so heavily upon so many of the people there. At one time people were employed at wages which would barely allow them to survive – 'We was starving against one another' as one needlewoman said in the middle of the last century. Mayhew, to whom she said this, also described her workshop.

> There was no table in the room; but on a chair without a back there was an old tin tray, on which stood a cup of hot milkless tea, and a broken saucer, with some half dozen small potatoes in it. It was the poor soul's dinner. Some tea-leaves had been given her, and she had boiled them up again to make something like a meal. She had not even a morsel of bread.[12]

Since then things obviously have changed, though tea-leaves are still boiled over again for second cups and tea-bags are used over and over again by people with little money. But real wages *have* risen, partly in response to the continuous pressure from trade unions whose fundamental purpose remains what it was when the Webbs wrote about them in *Industrial Democracy*,[13] the basis of association being sectional in nature. But the price of an increased standard of living has been a heavy one. Work has become in some ways less congenial, not so much in comparison with the early days of factory industry, when manufacturers like Robert Owen were few and far between, as in comparison with the period before the Industrial Revolution took off.

Growth of worker co-ops

If trade unions have continued to be the main expressions of solidarity, co-operatives have begun to reassert themselves in the last decade. It is true that co-operative retail societies have during that time been hard-pressed to hold on to a respectable share of the market. But in other sectors there has been growth. Agricultural and housing co-operatives have expanded. So in general have the worker co-operatives which are the subject of this book. As recently as 1976 there were some 47 worker co-operatives in the United Kingdom. By August 1982 nearly 500 were listed in the most recent *Directory* of the Co-operative Development Agency.[14] Currently the number is increasing by some five a week. The growth has admittedly been from a very low base and the number of members in all the co-ops belonging to the main support organization, the Industrial Common Ownership Movement (ICOM), is still not much more than 7,000 and the number of their employees (including members) not that much over 10,000, which compares with a figure of some 200,000 members of worker co-ops in another Common Market country, Italy. The British figure does not include all the co-operatives in existence and it does not include the John Lewis Partnership which we shall refer to later. Even so, worker co-operatives of all types are not yet of such a size as to constitute a challenge either to capitalism or to state socialism. But they could be eventually. The recent growth of worker co-operatives has continued to accelerate while the fortunes of the other two main sorts of business in the modern economy have been on the decline.

Most of the new ventures have not been in ordinary industry and building, where the main strength of European co-ops lies, but in services. Here are just a few of the new co-ops started in one month of 1982:

Co-operating Systems Co-op	Manchester	Computer consultants
Heritage Holidays Co-op	Wokingham	Travel agents
Totnes Communications Co-op	Totnes	Printing and type-setting
Airedale Thermal Insulation	Bradford	Loft insulation
TV Co-operation	London	Programme producers
Corntek	Wales	Electronic engineers
Linlithgow Enterprises	Linlithgow	Wire winding

The balance has, however, been changing since 1980, with building and ordinary industry becoming more prominent. Even in these two categories most of the new co-ops are small – or, perhaps one should say, *still* small, since most of them are of such recent origin. Scott Bader is the only full co-op which is of medium size, with a workforce of some 500.

By and large co-ops in Britain are in industries and services which do not need a great deal of capital. This is shown by the same CDA *Directory*. It gives the numbers of co-ops in different areas of trading activity.

WORKER CO-OPERATIVES ACCORDING TO TRADE

Retail, distributive, catering and food processing	151
Printing and publishing	75
Building; house renovation and decoration; cleaning; waste recycling; architecture; gardening services	69
Record, film and music making; theatre; theatrical agencies; leisure	46
Engineering; electronics; chemicals; general manufacturing	41

Crafts; arts; carpentry, furniture-making and joinery	40
Advisory; consultative; educational and office services	33
Footwear, clothing and textile manufacture	32
Workspaces; umbrella co-operatives	15
Provision and hire of transport; bicycle and motor vehicle repairs	13

Reasons for growth

The most striking fact, however, is the growth in numbers and, even more, in interest. Why should it have happened? To answer that we need to start with the traditional case for co-operatives.

The first thing to say is that co-operatives have always been seen as an alternative to private ownership, but not of consumer goods. Mr Smith as an owner has an almost uncontested right to enjoy the use of his house or car or TV set or lawn mower or paintbrush and within the law to do what he likes with them, free from interference by anyone else. That kind of ownership is as readily intelligible as it is readily defensible.

What is in dispute is the private ownership of the means of production. Mr Smith does not exercise power over others through his ownership of his car or his TV set, unless it be over his wife and children; or they over him. But when Mr Smith acts for the owners, or is both owner and manager, of a factory, or an office, or a fleet of trucks he exercises power not only over things but over the people who are employed in them. He can in large measure (even in a society where the unions are so strong) determine what they do for the part of their lives they contract to him. How that power should be exercised has been a subject of almost continuous debate since the Industrial Revolution. At that time the family stopped being the main unit of production on the land. Up till the Industrial Revolution almost all employment was self-employment, or at any rate family employment.

Since then private enterprise – the words are greatly misused – has increasingly given way to collective enterprise in the form of companies. The employer has ceased to be an individual and become a corporate body and the dominant corporate body has become a large one. The commanding heights of the economy (to use Lenin's phrase which has retained its popularity) are held by large national and multi-national companies and nationalized industries, and in all of these as we said in the Introduction the power is not held by the owners so much as by professional managers paid to act on their behalf.

This leaves many managers very much on their own, only nominally accountable to shareholders as long as the dividends can be kept flowing. Their accountability is in other words a kind of fiction. As long as they can keep out the legislators and liquidators and fend off take-over bids they can do very much what they like. To their employees it seems that much of what they do is calculated very shrewdly, to advance their own interests.

The 'class struggle' is not just something that Karl Marx wrote about: it is part and parcel of the everyday experience of most workers, with the conflict not being between them and the owners but between them and the managers. Staff and employees or managers and workers, whether or not they occupy separate buildings (as is common), are often marked out by their dress like officers and men in the armed services but in a way that fits industry – staff wearing their ordinary clothes and employees overalls or the like; by their car-parks – staff having their own, nearer the offices where they sit; by the conditions in which they work' – offices for the officers on the one hand which are not much less comfortable than their sitting rooms at home, and for the top people offices often literally at the top of the building; by their shorter hours of work and by the times at which they arrive at work and, perhaps above all, by the meals they eat at the company's expense. The power of the company car is aligned with the power of the executive in the organization, and for the people in the cars there are private medical care, help with private schooling, top-hat pension schemes, houses and even sometimes company suits to wear out on the company upholstery.

The resulting division between the two sides has been described by Robert Oakeshott.

From the management side, if what I have seen myself is any guide, it is experienced as an almost unbearable atmosphere of conflict, suspicion and mistrust. It is as if the shop floor's objectives were not only structurally different from, but in almost direct opposition to, those of management and of the long-term strength of the enterprise. Certainly I have found that the mistrust and suspicion across this 'interface' is at least as powerful as any between white and black in post-colonial Africa.[15]

The plea from advocates of co-operation is that to alter such an atmosphere of conflict managers should not take decisions about their own perks or indeed about anything else that deeply affects the interests of all the employees without being more fully accountable for these decisions than they are at the moment. Make the employees into the owners and managers would be accountable to owners who were not absentees but very much on the spot.

Stagflation

The criticism of this sort of management is of long standing. What has given it a special edge is the emergence of inflation – or rather the dreadful combination of inflation and unemployment sometimes called stagflation – as the central problem of the modern economy. It is a disease of the whole Western world but with Britain being at a more advanced stage of it. The problem has been made a great deal more severe by the constant pressure for wages to be increased faster than production. The unions are forever trying, quite justifiably from the point of view of their sectional interest, to protect their members from inflation by gaining increases as near as possible large enough to offset the actual or expected increases in prices. If they succeed, their members' standard of living will be kept stable. But for the country generally the attempt further undermines the economy. If prices are expected to rise by 10 per cent and wages consequently go up by 10 per cent while the production of goods and services remains static, prices are bound to jump. The rise in unit costs will see to that. The expectation becomes self-fulfilling.

The Thatcher Government has used only one blunt instrument to try and control this spiralling inflation. Monetarism has been the theory, unemployment has been the weapon, intended to reduce the bargaining power of the trade unions and hence their capacity to push up wages. It is a cruel policy which has sent unemployment to the highest level for fifty years. Historians will almost certainly pronounce it a disastrous failure.

Incomes policies of one kind or another are the only alternative and for the most part any government committed to them is going to have to operate them within the structure of industry as it exists now. But so far none of these policies, however successful for a period in restraining wage increases, has lasted. Without a rather fundamental reorganization of industry it will always be difficult to make incomes policies stick. Hence the new interest, amongst economists and others, in co-operatives. They offer a solution which has not yet been tried for one of our most severe economic problems.

The argument runs like this. A co-operative is formed by workers who get together and form collectives to own and run enterprises. There are no employees any more, only employers. The workers hire capital instead of being hired by it. They stand to get any profit they may be able to make; if they make a loss they also run the risk of losing any money they have put into the business and also their jobs. In principle, being owners, they can only remunerate themselves out of any surplus they succeed in making after all costs have been covered apart from wages. As the owners of the business they are entitled to the residual, what is left over, just as the capitalist owners are, or think themselves to be. At Mondragon (to which we will come later in this chapter) the fact of worker ownership in a co-operative is recognized by calling the wage an *anticipo*, something paid in anticipation of there being a favourable residual at the end of the year.

Practice will not, of course, be quite like that. The members of a co-operative have to live. They have to be paid wages. They cannot, like wealthy capitalists, wait until the end of a year and only then take whatever the profits justify. But in setting their wage levels they are likely to have a different attitude if they own the business themselves. When the business is owned by someone else, with that someone else often enough thought to be stashing away profits which could be much better used to elevate wages, there is no reason for workers to accept responsibility for the welfare of the enterprise as a whole. Get as much as you can seems to be a perfectly good rule. But transfer the ownership to the workers and they are much more likely to accept that they would be foolhardy to do as ordinary employees try to do, that is set their wages in advance at levels which it may not be possible to afford. If they do so set them they will at least have to be flexible and allow rates to fall or rise according to the success of the business. Wage rates could not be pushed up faster than the level of production without the jobs and interest of members being put at risk; and, that being so, the wage–cost–price spiral should in time become a thing of the past.[16] The consequences of pushing up wages faster than productivity would not be borne by someone else, at least prospectively; they would rest on the shoulders of the people who did the pushing.

Without success in this effort democracy itself may not survive. Peter Jay is one economist and supporter of co-operatives who believes the stakes are as high as that.

> But if those who basically believe that individuals must predominate over organizations, that man should be master of the machines and institutions which he has created, and all join hands to demand a restoration of the sovereignty of the consumer in the market-place over an extended area of national life and at the same time to demand the sovereignty of the members of an enterprise within it, then the electorate might yet be offered a way out of catastrophe without suspension of political freedoms.[17]

Another economist to have written in the same general vein is Nobel prize-winner James Meade.

> Against this background the workers in each individual co-operative would receive whatever they could earn. There would no longer be a situation in which an explosive inflation was threatened by workers pressing for a rise in money wages that represented a rise in real standards that exceeded the rise in productivity. They would, as the entrepreneurs, take in the form of the earned surplus whatever their productive efforts achieved. . . . Labour co-ops are designed to get rid of the conflict between 'them' and 'us', between 'owners or bosses' on the one hand and 'workers' on the other hand. It is for this reason that their institution may be advocated as a means of coping with the problem of explosive inflationary wage pressures. There no longer exists the possibility of pushing 'our' wages up in order to capture some of 'their' profits.[18]

Despite his support Meade utters some warnings, especially if co-ops form monopolies. He is very much opposed to 'natural' monopolies like gas or electricity supply being run by worker co-ops. For their members could, like any other monopolists not subject to control, do much as they wished with their prices and exploit consumers accordingly, just as they could if they captured a private monopoly. Meade even argues that a co-op monopoly would be more restrictive than a capitalist monopoly. The co-op might be willing to take in new members only if its monopoly profit were, by doing so, increased at least in proportion to the increase in the size of the membership – if the monopoly profit were increased less than that the additional workers would not bring in enough extra to pay their own wages unless these were less than those of the existing members. If they did not bring in that amount extra the wages of the existing members would have to be reduced. A capitalist in a similar situation would not be so motivated. He would be satisfied if the employment of extra people raised his monopoly profit at all, and to this end would take on people at lower wages than the rest of his employees (which he is assumed to have the freedom to do) as long as his own profits were even marginally raised in consequence.

Since it has to be accepted that co-op members are not, and will not be, any more saintly than anyone else, it has also to be accepted – paradoxical though it may sound – that co-ops need as much as any other kind of concern to operate within a framework of competition. Then they would not be able to gang up against consumers if they were tempted to do so. The Monopolies Commission would still be needed in the co-operative commonwealth. Given that basic safeguard, Meade inclines very much towards worker co-ops as have many others who fear that stagflation may yet destroy the economies of the world.

We began this chapter by juxtaposing co-operation and competition, and made it clear where in general terms our preference lay. But on the point raised by Meade we would be very much with him, while fully admitting the force of the paradox. Competition does have its uses as a means of controlling power, whether it is conferred by a monopoly in industry or by a monopoly in government. Britain's experience with nationalized monopolies has certainly made the competition between producers more attractive than it used to seem to people who were more naturally followers of Robert Owen than of Adam Smith – so much so, indeed, that it has now to be allowed that if there are to be many more co-operatives (as we hope there will be) none of them should be given or should take the kind of monopoly power state industries have had. They should be required to compete with the private and the public sector as well as with each other.

Failure of nationalization

Another reason for the growth in popularity of co-operatives has been the decline in popularity of state ownership. This other form of common ownership exercised through the state carried almost all before it for some years after the war, partly because the unions wanted it that way. Although, as we shall see later in this book, the attitude of unions has begun to change, for a long period they have been out of sympathy with co-operatives, favouring nationalization instead. Unions are mostly large national bodies. Many of their leaders preferred to deal with state-run industries also run on a large scale, and with the resources of the taxpayer behind them, than with a lot of co-operatives, the majority of them being small. State socialism has suited them better than co-operative socialism.

In its time nationalization also seemed a very neat solution to the problem of accountability raised earlier. In such industries the line of accountability seems to be firm and clear, if in two steps – from managers to the 'state' in the form of Ministers and from Ministers to the elected representatives of the people in Parliament to whom the nationalized industries should be mainly answerable. Unfortunately it has not worked out as the unions, or anyone else, hoped it would. The executive power has been with the managements. But they have always had to deal with Whitehall in a relationship which has always been fraught, with the executives complaining that the Ministers and their civil servants try to interfere so much as to make their jobs almost impossible. The relationship between Whitehall and Parliament has also been a constant irritation to both sides, with Whitehall on the whole enjoying continuous success in keeping effective power away from Parliament. The nationalized industries (when coupled with their controlling Departments of State) have been models, but only of what *not* to do.

This is particularly so because the methods of management have left no place for worker participation of the kind that was once hoped for. The traditional aim was, as Ken Coates has pointed out, workers' control, meaning management of the industries by the workers.[19] Clause 4 of the Labour Party Constitution when it was drafted in 1918 by the cautious hand of Sidney Webb, himself the enemy of guild socialism, did not appear to go as far as that when it called for the means of production, distribution and exchange to be transferred to common ownership (as it was called before 'public ownership' became the usual term) and thereafter to be subject to the 'best obtainable system of popular administration and control'. The language shows that words do not have to be as ringing as the Gettysburg Address or Gladstone's words in the Midlothian campaign in order to have a hold upon the loyalties of men, not in Britain anyway. 'Popular' was the kind of ambiguous word that Webb would have liked. Yet popular control was for many years interpreted to mean workers' control in a straightforward sense that Webb was all against. Remove the capitalist, remove the exploiter who treated 'labour' as though it were a commodity rather than a human being, remove this supreme irritant, put the workers in control, make them responsible for managing the affairs of industry and (ran the argument) a new spirit of fraternity, the same binding force that has held the unions together, would surely hold sway in industry too. The conflict in that cockpit derives from different relationships to property, on the one hand the managers representing the propertied interest in industry and on the other the workers with nothing to sell but their labour. Give the state the ownership and the workers control and that searing conflict would surely disappear. This belief was as important in inspiring the Russian Revolution in 1917 as it was the victory of the Labour Party in 1945.

Today, the view seems naive. The progressives who sought

29

for new and more constructive relationships between people at work have now had several decades of hard experience to learn from. Nationalization in the Soviet Union has buttressed tyranny; nationalization in Britain has done nothing to reduce conflict in industry. If anything, there is more bitterness amongst employees in the state than in the private sector. This has been evident for a long time, although not yet long enough to force a change of mind in the Labour Party, tied as it is to its past, that is to Clause 4 and to the acts of nationalization which have followed from it. But the basic demand for 'workers' control' is no less appealing today than it ever was. In some ways it is more so. In this sphere 'socialism' need not be the creature of the state. Ownership in particular, need not be suspended uneasily between Whitehall and the House of Commons, but vested in the people who actually do the work. We are not pretending that conflict between managers and workers will be removed at a stroke by such means. After so many disappointments it would be ridiculous to be millenarian about *any* new approach, or the revival of *any* old approach. But at least worker co-operatives offer a good deal more hope of introducing a new spirit into industrial life than do either of the two main institutions tried so far. If co-operatives are the contemporary manifestation of the ideas underlying Guild Socialism and workers' control, they are all the better for that.

Alternative movement

The cumulative case made so far has been far-reaching enough. But even more radical claims than that are being made for co-operatives, not by economists nor even by those trade unionists who have clung to the desirability of workers' control, but by people who have joined co-ops like SUMA described in the last chapter. They have, incidentally, brought a more pronounced middle-class element into workers' co-ops than at any time since Kingsley, Maurice and Neale and the other Christian Socialists of the last century were so impressed with the co-operative workshops set up in Paris in the course of the 1848 revolution that they determined to emulate them in Britain.

The twentieth-century recruits are as much influenced by

unemployment and inflation as anyone else. But many of those who join the alternative movement are reacting against more than that. They would be opposed to the existing order even if it were in tune, and full employment and stable prices components of it. Their criticism is of the whole of modern society, or at any rate a good span of it. The growth in their number is yet another reason for the spurt in co-operation in recent years.

To call it a 'movement' may suggest a homogeneity it does not possess. Its adherents are, by the nature of their beliefs, keener on each individual's manifesto than on collective ones. All the same, many of them share some distinctive characteristics and distinctive beliefs. They are, for instance, mostly young and hopeful that they can establish an alternative way of life instead of following their parents either onto the dole or into the kind of humdrum job that used to be acceptable. There is much about such humdrum jobs that they criticize. To put up with them for the sake of the money they will bring is to condemn people to degrading toil which can never be compensated for by the goods that the money will buy. Frustration at work is bound, they say, to spread over into the rest of life: people cannot isolate themselves from it by a barrier of money. It is, rather, likely to produce a restless acquisitiveness which expresses itself in an endless and endlessly unsatisfying quest for a higher 'standard of life', which turns out to be a dog's life rather than a full life. They also want to feel that the goods or services they produce are worthwhile in themselves, that they satisfy some need that matters and not just a titillation or a distraction produced because it makes a profit in a world whose values have become distorted. Profits there have to be to sustain a continuing business, but they should not be the primary goal so much as the secondary result of doing something that is worthwhile in more fundamentally human terms. The cheap and the gimcrack can never generate any pride in work.

Useful things must be produced; in other ways too the work involved must be less cramping to the spirit. The aim is that workers should as far as possible control their own lives, not be controlled in them by others. Individuals should, for example, be more free than they are to choose their own hours rather than being lockstepped into a timetable devised by someone else from which there is no escape. They have to arrive at someone else's 8 and leave not before someone else's 4.30. This may be conducive to efficiency of a kind. If so, it is a sort of efficiency which many people attached to the movement are prepared to forego. They would rather opt for some variant of flexitime so that – even though earnings may be lower as a result – they become more their own people. In sum, they want more individual autonomy such as they can get (to some extent) in a co-operative. For some of them co-operative management is the only legitimate art of the many arts of management. In such a framework they can hope to achieve rather more fairness than is usually attained – not just in the distribution of power, but in incomes, and between the sexes.

A co-operative way of working and living is not by any means the only aspiration of the people who seek an alternative lifestyle. But it is an important component all the same and has helped to create a whole new wing for orthodox co-operatives. This has not occurred in Britain on the same scale as in West Germany, where there may be as many as 350,000 members of, and, sympathizers with, the alternative movement, with the *Self-help Network* at its centre.[20] The phenomenon which in this chapter we have been attempting to explain is concerned not just with work but with the whole of life.

The two weaknesses

If these are the background reasons for the recent growth of co-operatives the puzzle is why that growth has not been still more spectacular than it has been. So much has been operating in favour of co-operatives. Why are they not by now dominating the economy? There is prejudice against them, to be sure. In many quarters co-ops are bad news, partly because *the* co-op is the store in the High Street and this no longer has the overwhelming appeal of the shop in Toad Lane, to put it mildly.

But there are deeper causes than that, which were as it happens identified nearly a century ago in a statement by Beatrice Potter (later Mrs Webb) which has itself become part of the history of co-operation in Britain and, since the book was as well as being read so widely in English translated into many other languages, in the world as well.[21] The arguments in it were brought out and dusted over again in a later book of which Sidney Webb was the joint author; this was written in order to discredit the Guild Socialism to which they were so implacably hostile and which seemed at the time to be bonding shop stewards and intellectuals into a dangerous compact.[22]

Mrs Webb was as cold towards producer societies as she was warm towards consumer ones. This was due partly to her (and her husband's) belief that the proper function of trade unions was to protect their members from being exploited by owners and managers, and that they should not be distracted from it by also assuming some of the responsibility of managers – a view which has had many modern proponents[23] and has indeed become the orthodoxy of the trade union movement. They should stick to their last, and not meddle with matters of production, these being the sphere of professional management.

The Webbs had a pluralist view of democracy, at least until they were bowled over by the good order (on paper) of Soviet Communism in the 1930s.[24] A pluralist democracy as they saw it needed not just an ordinary parliament, that is not just political democracy; it also needed an industrial democracy, this being the sphere of the unions, and a consumer democracy embodied in consumer co-operatives. Democracy in general, nourished by the separation of powers between the separate democracies, could always be threatened by their unification. That much of the argument we would accept, certainly not wanting trade unions to abandon their ordinary functions inside worker co-operatives, although we would as certainly hope to see some change in the manner in which they are performed.

But one can hold that position without doing what Mrs Webb did and condemning producer co-operatives as a consequence. She thought they could not possibly succeed for long, particularly if the unions would listen to her (as they have done, without perhaps knowing it) and abandon any interest they might have in workers' control. The shortcomings were too great. She picked out two main weaknesses, which, it has to be admitted, are still there. The first was, and is, shortage of capital. Even the consumer societies she commends have been plagued by it. 'The Store accumulates capital at a snail's pace.' But this was not so critical for distribution as it was for manufacturing industry which could only bear up against competition if each worker was supported by a large amount of capital equipment. That co-operatives should want to produce for use, not profit, was fine ethically, but less so economically. The workers, being workers, could not supply enough of their own capital, and yet they could not expect to attract outside loans from individual profit-seekers and from a financial community which looked to Adam Smith for its credo, if it looked at all.

That would not have mattered so much but for the second weakness, the low calibre of the management of producer societies. If management had been good, good money would have followed it. But it had not been good – hence, she said, the many failures in these societies in the nineteenth century. The producer societies were confronted by a contradiction from which they could find no escape. On the one hand they had, as democracies, to subordinate management to the individual workers who were the co-operative's members. This was their reason for existing at all. But on the other hand to survive in a competitive economy they needed management which would be just as effective as that of their capitalist rivals. According to Mrs Webb, they could not, or at any rate in the nineteenth century did not, enjoy management of that kind. How could they, when a manager who had throughout the day been examining the work of his committee-men, fixing their piece-rates, disciplining them for their mistakes and oversights, controlling the way in which they used their time, had, come the evening, to put up with a change of scene and reversal of relations? 'The manager stands as a servant before the board of directors.' They may decide to discipline him if he tries to discipline them. 'Consider a railway managed on the system of the porters choosing the station master, the station master choosing the traffic superintendent, the whole body of employees choosing the board of directors!'[25] The exclamation mark was hers.

The criticism has kept its point. Many co-operatives clearly have suffered from weak management. This became a matter of common knowledge – notoriety to the enemies of co-ops – when the 'Wedgie Benn' co-ops were set up in the 1970s and substantial public money was injected into the *Scottish Daily News*, the

Meriden plant making motorcycles and Kirkby Manufacturing and Engineering (KME) in Liverpool making storage heaters and the like. Of those only Meriden has survived, after many ups and downs.

The only one of the three as yet fully reported is KME. Tony Eccles has written an excellent account of it. Poor management was certainly one of the principal causes of its eventual failure. The two shop stewards, Jack Spriggs and Dick Jenkin, who had led the initial protest against the closure of the factory became the chief managers, in fact if not in name. They were, as Mrs Webb was no doubt noticing from her grave, unable to impose on the workers any more disicipline (if that) than the previous managers and they had no experience whatsoever in the practice of management only in opposing it. In some respects their power was less. Since the co-operative had been brought into existence in order to save jobs on Merseyside they felt they could not sack anyone even when they knew (as almost everyone did) that the factory was overmanned. They also bore out what Mrs Webb had said about trade unions in a co-operative. It was evidently a mistake to have 'single-channel' control without a distinction being made between the shop steward structure and the management structure. The central dilemmas were those arising from the dual role of the convenor-directors held by the two leading shop stewards.

> People had no way of protesting at management decisions which had been initiated or agreed by the directors; management felt threatened and uneasy at being responsible to on-site directors who were ostensibly non-management yet who actively managed the enterprise; it was never clear whether Jack and Dick were acting as directors or as convenors.[26]

Example of Mondragon

Whether or not Mrs Webb can be convincingly resurrected as the theoretician of KME, the guardian of her true gospel against Wedgwood Benn, the fate of the famous three associated with him was not exactly helpful to the cause. We said earlier that the association with *the* co-op, in the High Street, was a liability for some people, and to that, in the 1970s, had to be added these further liabilities in Glasgow, Liverpool and Meriden. But to offset them there has appeared, from the most unlikely quarter, the Basque provinces of Spain, another example of co-operative practice which has been increasingly talked about and points rather firmly in the other direction. We are, of course, referring to Mondragon.

Mondragon has shown that worker co-operatives are not after all cursed by any Webbian inevitability which makes them bound to fail. There they have succeeded and done so consistently. Exceeding by far the hopes of the Catholic priest, Father Arizmendi, who had the original conception in the 1940s, the Mondragon co-operatives have on all manner of counts out-performed comparable capitalist industry in Spain.[27] They have raised the standard of education in a whole region of their country by the schools and colleges they have supported and stimulated in a way which would have delighted the Pioneers. They have raised the quality of life through the flourishing housing co-operatives, health co-operatives and consumer co-operatives associated with them.

Robert Oakeshott has done more than anyone else to publicize them in Britain.[28] As he has shown, the Mondragon co-operatives have expanded steadily in the quarter of a century since the first of them was founded. By the 1980s there are within the one network some 150 worker co-ops employing some 18,000 people. None of the individual co-operatives has failed (apart from one in fishing), even in the recession which has put strains as great on the Spanish economy as it has on the British. No one has been made redundant. Wages are higher than in the Basque region generally. This is partly because many of the co-ops are in relatively high-tech industries, like machine tools, refrigerators and other domestic appliances, electrical plant, agricultural machinery and precision micro-mechanics.

All this they have done by avoiding both of the weaknesses the Webbs identified with the help of a new kind of institution in the co-operative firmament, their own bank, the Caja Laboral Popular, dedicated to the support of worker co-ops. Such a bank specializing in giving support of the most wide-ranging kind to worker co-operatives is an advantage that British societies have never had. It is a savings bank for the region and some of these savings have been used to create jobs. People are more ready to put their savings into the bank because they approve of its object, job-creation.

The bank, by adding to the capital which each member of a co-operative is as an individual required to invest in it, has ensured that none of the co-operatives has lacked for capital and hence for the equipment that would endow them as well as, or better than, any of their competitors. The Webbs did not even conceive of a bank acting as the promoter and co-ordinator of a network of producer societies. If they had they could well have taken a much less gloomy view of their prospects.

The Caja must also be given some of the credit for the firmness of management. All co-ops must in exchange for capital and other services employ the Caja as their banker and supply it with regular information about their progress. If there is any falling back in sales or profitability from month to month the Caja can then take instant action. Financial discipline is tight.

The Caja also helps to train managers and to advise them when they are selected or re-selected by the individual members in each separate co-operative. Then it has in its Empresarial (or consultancy) Division a first-class back-up service with a staff of over a hundred experts. Every co-op has a 'godfather' from the Empresarial who keeps in regular touch with it. Whenever any problem arises the individual co-op can turn to its godfather for guidance. Power is decentralized inside the Mondragon group right down to the level of the individual member; equally there is a great deal of strength at the centre which can be and is used in the interests of each individual co-op and of the collectivity of all of them. The result of the Caja presence and of the enviable reputation of Mondragon is that the quality of managers they attract is notably high.

Their managers have demonstrated that what the Webbs thought an absurdity – 'The whole body of employees choosing the board of directors' – is not necessarily one at all. Mondragon managers have an authority which many capitalist managers would envy, being the more so because it rests on a basis of consent even though the election of managers is indirect. All workers taken together make up the General Assembly of each co-operative. The General Assembly elects the *Junta Rectora*, the governing but non-executive board, and this in its turn appoints the management. The relationships are shown in Figure 1.

We shall have more to say about this experiment at later points in the book. For the moment all we want to do is to record the effect which Mondragon has had on informed opinion since it became well-known and the evidence it has provided against the Webb thesis. It is a thesis still subscribed to by many people inside and outside British industry, who, if they have ever heard of this Basque project at all, may be rather unclear as to what sort of dragon it is.

Conclusion

To recapitulate, we have in this chapter not been setting out in brief compass yet another interpretation of the history of the labour movement so much as putting worker co-operatives, and especially their recent return to favour, into an historical context. They arose in the nineteenth century, as part of the self-help movement launched by and for the working classes before the state came to their aid in the twentieth century. The movement had three arms, in co-operatives, unions and parties, namely the Labour Party in conjunction with the Co-operative Party.

Of the three, trade unions have for a hundred years at least been the most powerful in the labour trinity. They have determined the direction taken by the whole movement, in doing so leaning sometimes towards one of their partners and sometimes towards the other. Their attachment to the co-operatives – and more broadly to the tradition that it is 'the poor what helps the poor' – was one of the reasons for the support they gave to workers' control at various stages in the history of the movement. Workers' control would have implied direct action and the acceptance of responsibility for running institutions instead of acting solely as an official opposition which (unlike Her Majesty's Opposition) would never have to take power.

But opposition it has been (so far anyway) and the unions made their alliance not with the co-operatives and their old tradition but with the Labour Party and its old tradition. The

Item Issued

Camilla Mary Salisbury

0 0 2 1 0 7 7 4 7 3

Student

Due 26/03/2012 23:59

Co-operative opportunity / The UK Cooperative Council.

334 COO

9 0 0 2 1 3 2 7 1 7

Item Issued

Camilla Mary Salisbury

Student

Due 10/04/2012 23:59

Building communities the
co-operative way / Johnston
Birchall; foreword by Michael
Young.
Birchall, Johnston.
334.1 BIR

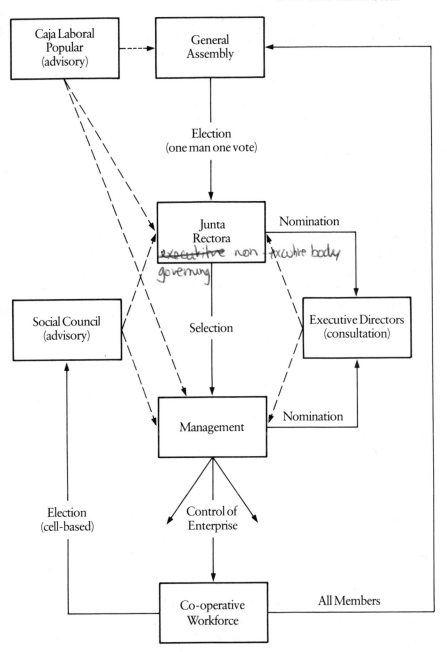

Figure 1. Organization chart of a Mondragon Co-operative

collectivist sentiments that were generated in the Victorian period and persisted afterwards found expression not through co-operatives but through the party. The demand for workers' control led to common ownership by the state rather than by the workers themselves; about the outcome, though we are of course biased, we do not think that many people would rejoice. Nationalization has hardly been a wild success. This route to workers' control has turned out to be a cul-de-sac.

Could there be another way? And could it be the co-operative way? Almost any economic historian would answer in the negative. Owen, he might well say, was a more persuasive advocate for co-operatives than any there have been since, being himself what few of the modern advocates are, a manager with a golden record. He, with all his authority, called for co-operatives and what did he get, then or later? A great deal of excitement. A great deal of talk. And not much action. Worker co-operatives had a headstart on the limited liability company and since Owen's time worker co-operatives have had 150 years or more to prove him right.

That they have not done so on any large scale, not yet anyway, is no doubt due to the two Webb weaknesses, and to much else. Given the experience so far, why should there be a better chance in the rest of this century than there has been in the last two? We shall be looking at this central question from several different points of view in the chapters that follow. Meanwhile, let us just say that the outlook is better for the reasons given earlier in this chapter. These have produced a significant response from two quarters in particular.

First, many more middle-class people have come in as enthusiasts than at any other period. The Owens are not counted in small numbers this time and the new influx includes many more people than those we have already mentioned who would think of themselves as belonging to the alternative movement. They are different from the Christian and the Guild Socialists in that they are not so much calling on others to act as acting themselves, as members and sometimes as managers of co-operatives. Robert Oakeshott has traced the failure of co-ops to grow and prosper to their 'cloth cap' character in Britain, and the success of Mondragon to their appeal for engineers and managers as well as for the Spanish equivalent of our cloth caps. If he is right, then the incapacity is a good deal less than it has been at any time since the formation of the Grand National Moral Union of the Productive Classes.

The second response has been from some trade unionists. Nationalization has been a disappointment to many of them, as it has to their middle-class allies. Workers' control does not lie in nationalization or even, at a lower level, in shared participation in management. If that is so, might the unions turn away from their commitment to the state and to Labour politics, with all the disappointments they have brought, and towards a modern form of workers' control? It is, of course, always easier to drift than to paddle. But it is at least possible that the unions will before too long desert their entrenched position of permanent opposition in industry, and the lack of responsibility which goes with it. There are already some strange portents. This kind of news story would have been unthinkable even ten years ago:

> The first trade-union-sponsored co-operative in Britain yesterday celebrated one year in business with a confident statement that it was now making money and might even employ more people next year. The statement came from Moss Evans, General Secretary of the Transport & General Workers' Union, to a delighted audience of workers and friends in the cutting room which also serves as the canteen of the Taunton Shirt Co-operative. A celebration cake was cut, and the staff enjoyed drinks provided by a local cider company.[29]

It must be clear from the way we have presented our argument that a conclusion on these lines is one we wish for, and that it could amongst other things take the form of a commitment on the part of the unions to a modernized version of workers' control, or Guild Socialism for that matter, such as the version found at Mondragon. In that case there would again be some leaning towards the third partner, the co-operative movement, and towards the third sector which it must be the aspiration of the co-operative movement to build, or to re-build.

3   What is a worker co-operative?

The most recent authoritative definition of a worker co-operative comes from the International Co-operative Alliance, the worldwide body which represents co-operatives of all types, agricultural, consumer, credit, housing, worker. In 1966 the ICA brought the original Rochdale formula up to date, in the form of six principles which were intended to embrace all the kinds of co-operatives in the ICA, including those to which this book is devoted.

A co-operative is, then, a group of people who join together in a common undertaking such that:

a) membership is voluntary and open;
b) there is democratic control, usually on the basis of one member, one vote;
c) interest on share capital is limited;
d) there is equitable distribution of any surplus or savings among the members;
e) provision should be made for education of their members, officers and employees and of the general public in the principles and techniques of co-operation;
f) co-operatives co-operate in every practical way with other co-operatives at local, national and international levels.

As for the practice, this of course varies. There is in Britain a Registrar responsible for the implementation of the Industrial and Provident Societies Acts. These were drafted in their original form partly by E.V. Neale, the Christian Socialist secretary of the Co-operative Union and one of the protagonists of producer co-ops in the great debates of the 1870s and 1880s on consumer versus producer control.[30] If the Registrar or some official body were the only interpreter of the six principles there might be more agreement about their meaning. His or its constitutional rules would be *the* rules. This is what happens in many other countries where there is one main federation or support organization for worker co-ops, such as the Confédération Générale des SCOP (Sociétés Co-opératives Ouvrières de Production) in France. But in Britain there have been four main bodies which offer model rules, acceptable to the Registrar, to any group of people who want to save themselves the cost, trouble and time of devising their own tailor-made ones. The four, which we will refer to later on by their initials alone, are the Co-operative Union incorporating the old CPF (Co-operative Productive Federation), ICOM (Industrial Common Ownership Movement), CDA (Co-operative Development Agency) and JOL (Job Ownership Ltd). We will come back to these bodies in Chapter 5. For the moment, in elaborating the six principles we will show only how far they agree on them and how, on the contentious issue of individual or collective shareholding, they differ.

Voluntary and open membership

There is not much room for conflict about voluntary membership. No one (outside communist countries) can be compelled to join a co-operative against his will. Compulsory co-operation is almost a contradiction in terms. But there is a question about whether anyone working for a co-operative should (after a probationary period) be compelled to join as a member and not continue just as an employee. On this practice varies. Open membership means that all workers should be eligible to join. This is accepted by all the four bodies. If this were not so it would be possible for a group of members to close the doors once they had passed through themselves and consign all later arrivals to second-class citizenship. It would also be possible for members to exploit the non-members, defenceless because they had no right to vote on anything; and pay them less than members doing an equivalent job. If power were confined to a minority this would hardly be better than an ordinary company whose shareholders may not mind (or know) if their workers are exploited as long as it all adds to the profits which go into their private bank accounts.

One member, one vote

On this also there is general agreement. The only differences are about the way in which democracy is supposed to work in practice. In a very small co-operative control can be exercised directly, by all the members in general meeting. In large co-ops this is impracticable. Authority has to be delegated and this is recognized in their practice, and indeed in that of many small co-ops as well. Professional managers are quite as necessary in a co-op of some size as they are in any successful business of an ordinary sort; this all the members cannot claim to be. They have, therefore, to elect their directors or officers, whatever they are called, in the same way as shareholders of an ordinary company elect their board of directors.

The crucial difference is that in a co-op the workers *are* shareholders. So the directors, who themselves often appoint a general manager, are in the end accountable to them. Another difference is that in an ordinary company the votes vary with the size of the shareholding – the owner of a million shares has a million times more votes than the owner of one – whereas in a co-operative even though a member had a million they would still count as one for voting purposes. If that were not the case there would be no point in setting up a co-operative in the first place: one member who accumulated extra shares could get to the point where he could outvote everyone else and then do with the co-operative whatever he wanted.

So far so good. There is not the same unanimity on who should have the vote – whether it has to be a worker or whether it can also be an outsider. ICOM and JOL restrict membership to workers. The CDA rules allow outsiders including corporate bodies to be members and the old CPF rules did the same. Many of the nineteenth-century CPF co-ops were linked to consumer societies and it seemed only common sense to encourage them to take shares in worker co-ops to add to their capital. If consumer societies could be admitted, so could trade unions and also individuals. Sometimes outsider control was pushed so far as to transform the co-operative completely. This happened to the Rochdale Co-operative Manufacturing Society which was established alongside the retail society set up by the Rochdale Pioneers. Indeed, their shop, as we said before, was started partly in the hope that they might accumulate enough money to finance what they wanted, self-employment in flannel weaving, just as a disabled persons' club might have a jumble sale to raise money for a bus. The Society did in fact run a textile mill very successfully. But outside shareholders were invited to finance a brand new building. Soon there were 1,400 shareholders, of whom no more than 200 were workers. Eventually all the committee members were outside shareholders and nothing but. The co-operative had been taken over, step by step.

Of course, not all productive societies suffered this fate. But in many of them the outsiders, even though there was strict adherence to the principle of one member, one vote, were said to have too much influence. In particular, they were suspected of being too open to an offer to buy the whole co-operative, lock, stock and barrel, at a figure which would yield a capital gain. Most of the CPF societies which have sold up in recent years have had outside shareholders.

Limited interest

The capital in a co-operative is quite different from that in an ordinary company. Shares in a co-op are not an equity, entitling their holders to share proportionately in profits, so that if profits are very large so are the dividends. The Pioneers and their followers were, and are, opposed to this practice because it invites members to make profitability their main aim irrespective of how it is achieved, for example by selling shoddy goods, by charging too high a price or by paying too little in wages. They were not against usury, like their medieval ancestors, but they were against anything other than a fixed and limited rate of return. The proper end of production is to sell useful products or services at reasonable prices and to produce them by such methods that satisfaction in work is enhanced.

But all the rules allow co-ops to borrow money. Banks can be paid for their loans or overdrafts at going rates, and outsiders and others also at rates with a ceiling on them. CDA co-ops, for instance, can pay up to 1 per cent and ICOM co-ops 3 per cent above bank base rates. To allow interest to be paid at such a level is to go some way towards paying commercial rates for capital obtained by means of loan.

Equitable distribution

According to the orthodox canon, bonuses can be paid, these being distinguished from dividends which are proportionate to the number of shares held. Bonuses are not a reward so much for investing money as for investing work. If this is recognized and annual bonuses paid out of any surpluses made are related to what people have earned in wages, then there is no objection.

A much sharper dispute is about a related question, whether there should be any distribution at all among members of a surplus which arises when a co-operative is wound up. The ICA principles are silent on this point. The 1966 Congress at Vienna defeated a proposal to rule out the disposal of residual assets to members which was argued for on the grounds that such a disposal would be contrary to the other principles they were in the course of agreeing.

In Britain ICOM is on this issue on one side of the fence, while on the other the CDA in its 1982 model rules and JOL in its rules are partially with the old CPF societies. The latter allowed members to sell their co-operative as a going concern, or the assets in it after a liquidation, and divide the proceeds between themselves. This happened in several cases. Bristol Printers, for instance, was wound up in 1977 after sixty-eight years of trading. The motive was obvious. The shares held by members were worth £1 each, which is what they were when first purchased and what they so remained, since there was no way of sharing in capital gains except by selling up. When this was done each £1 share suddenly appreciated twenty-eight times. The CPF itself, which had twenty-four £1 shares in the co-op, got a cheque for nearly £700 from the liquidator. The workers benefited to a similar extent and so did outside shareholders such as Co-operative Retail Services. It was the same story with Wigston Hosiers nearly twenty years before, where there were also substantial outside shareholdings. Since then modified versions of the CPF and CDA rules have been produced for promoters of co-ops who want to restrict membership to workers.

The rules of ICOM forbid such a share-out. When a co-operative is dissolved the proceeds have to be used for the support of co-operation in other ways, or passed to charities. In JOL the same rule applies to a proportion of a co-op's capital. Without this rule members might be tempted to sell up whenever their assets were worth more than the value of the shares, which they would almost always be in an ICOM co-op where no one has more than one £1 share. They would also be in conflict with the sixth principle. Co-operatives belong to a wider movement: it is their duty to help each other, when they go out of business as well as when they are in it. ICOM refers to its practice as belonging to the 'village green' concept. 'Like the village green or the city park people have the right to it as long as they live in the village or the city but they cannot combine to sell it for their own gain.'[31] On this point we ourselves agree with ICOM.

Education

The fifth principle, about devoting some of the funds to education, has a nice Victorian ring to it, but one still highly relevant. We imagine that members of most co-ops attached to any of the support bodies would agree in a general way even if their rules do not expressly provide for educational support. But many of them do not do very much about it in practice.

Inter co-op

The sixth principle about co-operation between co-operatives is as difficult to contest as it is easy to ignore. Worker co-ops do of course support each other, to some extent. But what stands out is not so much the amount of inter-co-op support in Britain as the paucity of it – far less for worker co-ops than for retail societies. We come back to this point in Chapter 5.

The two schools

We now come to the major matter on which there *is* disagreement between what might be called the individualist and collectivist schools, being a matter on which the six principles are silent. The question in one form is whether members should have one or more shares and (more important) whether their shares should entitle them to participate in the prosperity of the business. More fundamentally, the question is about human nature – about what human beings are like – and nothing can be more contentious that that. Will a co-op thrive better if the members regard it as a composite of individuals with individual interests or as a collective affair in which the common interest is all and in which individual interests are submerged? There is a powerful case each way.

Those who hold to the first school of thought warn that if failure is what is sought and permanent marginalization of co-ops on the fringes of the main economy then the best approach will certainly be to regard people as though they are unselfish creatures always prepared to sink their own interests for the sake of others. In their hard-headed way they assert that, whatever the rhetoric, members of co-ops are in the long run just as hard-headedly self-regarding. To imagine otherwise is moonshine.

This general stress on the selfishness which always (or almost always) co-exists with altruism is clearly not just theoretical: it has the most practical implications for the manner in which it is thought that co-ops should be set up and run. According to this school, workers should be required to have a sizeable personal capital stake in the co-op. They would then be more likely to think of it as their own and to exert themselves for it.

A good deal more follows from the same premise. Workers may be prepared to do without a share in the annual profit. They could not be expected to put much of their own money at risk and leave it happily alone in their co-op if its value remained just the same through thick and thin. In an age of inflation the value of their capital stake would be eroded year by year as prices rose. So they must be allowed to share in capital appreciation and have it reflected in the value of their shares if the co-op does well. They must also be allowed to cash in their shares according to an agreed formula. If they can never get enough of their money out they will never be prepared to put enough of it in.

This school makes a great deal of one of the main problems identified in the last chapter – the shortage of capital. The fact that co-ops cannot raise ordinary equity capital from outside investors limits them in a number of ways. If they have only a very small equity base they are limited also in the amount of fixed-interest loans they can raise. If outside equity has to be ruled out it is cutting off your nose to spite your face to restrict the amount of money members themselves are encouraged or required to put into their own concern as risk money or to make it unattractive for them to leave their money there once it is in.

A constant danger for a collectivist co-op is that the assumption about human nature upon which it is based, that members will strive best when they do so for the common good, may not be borne out in practice. The form of the co-op, as a collectivist organization, will not save it in substance if members do not behave in the way they are supposed to. Since they cannot by any means get at the capital even when they are old and retire, why should members bother to nurture it? If they are so minded, they can (behind the screen of a high-minded common ownership) minimize the proportion of profits that is ploughed back into the maintenance and building up of capital by maximizing their own take-out or take-home pay – this by the simple means of raising their wages or awarding themselves a hefty, an over-hefty bonus. Selfishness can destroy a co-op in this manner just as surely as by winding it up to secure its assets for personal gain. This has been pinpointed by some critics as the greatest single weakness of co-ops in Yugoslavia. If there can, in other words, be no sharing in capital appreciation it may be so tempting to pay large wages and bonuses that it is done even at the expense of the seedcorn. It is perhaps significant that the Mondragon co-ops do not pay cash-bonuses: the preservation of their capital base is too important for that.

Furthermore, if such capital as the members provide is all loan capital (as it must be in an ICOM co-op which limits each member to one share) the co-op is especially vulnerable for another reason. The fixed interest carried by loans is a fixed cost like any other; it is supposed to be paid just like any other current bill; and payment has to be *before* any surpluses are made and ploughed back into better equipment or even into reducing the overdraft at the bank. The merit of share capital which entitles its holders to a share of the profits is that the share only has to be paid out *if* there are profits, that is if the concern can afford it. Fixed interest payments, on the other hand, have to be made whether or not concerns can afford it, even if they have to close down as a consequence.

The case the other way is almost equally powerful. To stress the different financial interests of different members is, according to the collectivist school, to introduce into a co-op capitalist attitudes which are all too likely to destroy it in the end. To recognize ownership by individuals is to invite them to behave selfishly. They may put their money in (if, that is, they have any to start with) but if so will naturally want the right to withdraw it, and if that is granted then if at any time several members of the co-op decide to pull out they can destroy its capital base. They are liable to distribute too much of the profits between themselves and not plough enough back into the business. They may be much too ready to restrict entry of new members with the same rights as themselves because then they would have to share any capital gains. They would rather keep all such gains to themselves and so take on new people as employees rather than full members. They will be ready to sell up the whole co-op to a capitalist concern if by doing so they can make a substantial profit. The members of a collectivist co-op can, it is admitted, behave selfishly too, but at least the constitution and the objectives do not encourage it. The constitution leans against the self-regarding motives and that is surely as it should be.

So we should be fearful of the consequences of treating the members of co-operatives as though they are just like the shareholders of ordinary companies except that they happen also to work in them. A company in which all the shares are owned by employees with a financial stake of their own in its profitability, however much it may look like a co-operative to begin with, is only too likely to degenerate in the course of time into what is in effect if not in law much like an ordinary company. No matter that members' shares in the profits are linked to the work they have contributed (measured by the wages they have received) rather than to the size of their shareholdings. Restrictions can be placed upon members' rights to withdraw their money, for example, upon their retirement or upon leaving the co-op because of ill health. But, given that they have the right to a share which has accrued in their accounts and which is related to profitability, how are they to get out the money? Since they cannot sell shares to outsiders and still remain a co-op, they can only get the money from the co-op itself, which means that when they do its capital will be depleted. The pressure to allow in outside capitalists to make up for what has been taken out could then become almost irresistible.

One of the support bodies, ICOM, holds very closely to the second school of thought and asserts that such dangers can only be avoided by making co-ops as far as possible collective affairs. The vast majority that have been established in the last ten years belong to ICOM, and subscribe to one form or another of its model rules. These all provide for a purely nominal shareholding of one per member. The fear is, or one fear is, that even though people who subscribed for more shares than that would still have only one vote, it would be like building in a sort of inequality from the start.

The other support bodies recognize the force of the argument presented by the collectivist school but do not choose to take them as far as ICOM. JOL, in some ways at the opposite extreme, has been much influenced in this, like all British enthusiasts, by the example of Mondragon. For JOL the success can be explained by the fact that, though in itself a remarkable collective achievement, it has not adopted by any means the whole of the collectivist creed. Its constitution is regarded as a sensible compromise between the two opposing views. JOL's director explains the compromise in this way.

A balance needs to be struck. There must be substantial individual 'ownership' – otherwise the interests of individual worker-members will not be securely linked to those of the co-op. Moreover, this individual 'ownership' must, at the outset, be purchased, not acquired as a gift, otherwise there will be no psychological feeling of responsible ownership (otherwise, too, the open-door policy of job expansion will be undermined). Yet, on the other hand, there must be substantial and fully protected collective ownership. For, if not, the ability of the co-op to survive and progress will be weakened.[32]

The balance is struck partly by requiring members to find their own entry fee or capital contribution. A few years ago the minimum size stake in a new co-op was about £2,000, a sum which is said to be a good deal easier to put together in the Basque country, with its strongly entrenched tradition of saving, than it would be for many working people in Britain. The figure for joining an old co-op was half that.

Right from the start this contribution is considered as being divided into two parts, 80 per cent belonging to the individual and placed in his capital account, and 20 per cent, the indivisible part, which is collectively owned. Also into an individual's account goes his share of the profits. The rule is that 30 per cent of any net profits, after ploughing back on a large scale out of gross profits, should be spent on collective purposes, such as education, amenities, and support for other co-ops. The other 70 per cent (or not more than 70 per cent) may be divided between members in proportions determined by their income from work and also by their income from interest. When losses are incurred, at least 70 per cent of them must be debited to members' accounts. The amount lodged in capital accounts is revalued from time to time in the light of inflation to allow for capital gain.

If that was all there was to it, worker shareholders, replacing ordinary ones, would be more or less on all fours with them. The only incentives would be those of individual gain, if within the framework of co-operative working. But there *is* more to it than that, with some leaning in the other direction as well. People at Mondragon recognize the need to uphold the collective interest which is also their own individual interest. The more each co-op is built up, the safer people's jobs, especially in a time of adversity like the present. The force of that argument is recognized by laying it down that members cannot take money out of their capital accounts except on retirement, death or extreme compassionate grounds. Since the accounts are effectively blocked, by and large the capital stays in the business; this allows employment to increase and the businesses to grow. Moreover, the Mondragon shares are unlike orthodox capitalist shares in another way as well. Their value is mainly proportionate to work done, and not a market value.

These rules do not remove altogether the danger of capital depletion. The Mondragon co-operatives have been expanding very fast. They have attracted mainly young workers. The average age of the workforce is thirty-four. The current roll of pensioners is no more than 110.[33] What will happen when large numbers reach retirement age together? By the mid-1990s many more members will be coming up for retirement each year, although it is not expected to be until 2021 that a peak retirement figure of 835 people will be reached. But the joint capital could be run down all the same, and co-ops perhaps be closed in consequence. This danger is, of course, much discussed and some people believe that the practice in some Mondragon co-ops should be extended to all so that the 70 per cent of profits is not credited to members but is put instead to reserve. But if that happened another problem could arise: individual incentives could be weakened.

In general JOL has been impressed by the combination of selfishness and altruism embodied in the Mondragon model, and has allowed for both in the form of co-op it favours. Its model articles declare that 'teams of people work best if organized in ways which recognise both their individual and collective interest'. But British law, especially on taxes, is different from Spanish, and JOL has not been able to bring to life an exact reproduction. Their chosen instrument is a company with two classes of shares, collective shares (A) and individual voting shares (B). Each individual can have only one B share. Every year auditors produce a valuation of the assets. If they have risen, the B shares are credited with a proportion of the gain according to the earnings of their owners. Members who leave cannot get full value until the reserve fund is sufficiently large to allow that to happen. But when it is, B shares will be bought by the owners of the A shares, in effect the company itself.

Enervating effect

The dispute is not so much about detail as about an important general issue. The adherents of the two schools have taken up strong ideological positions which have now become shot through with discussion of the Mondragon structure. The Labour Party, for example, in a report produced by a Working Group in 1980, after some favourable words about Mondragon, considered the Basques had gone so wrong on what was to them the central question that 'this emphasis on individual rather than collective ownership makes the model unacceptable to the working group'.[34] Instead, the Labour Party proposed more draconian compulsion than has ever been used anywhere in a democracy, allowing the workers in any private firm to convert their company into a co-operative if they wished.

Contrary to stereotype, European and most other co-operators appear to be much less ideological than the British. They know (as we in Britain do also, despite our odd behaviour) that if co-operatives are to survive in a hostile world, in competition with the entrenched enterprises of the first and second sectors, they need to stand united. It has so far been difficult to achieve that kind of unity in practice.

To state our view, highly desirable as greater unity is, why cannot it be compatible with diversity? We said earlier that the protagonists are asking fundamental questions about human nature. But they are liable to produce pat answers. The crucial assumption of both seems to be that it is proper to think of it as an either/or matter, as if all people were either individualist or collectivist. If that was so, all that would have to be done would be to discover which people were which and design co-operatives (and indeed all other institutions) accordingly.

Surely that is far too simple. Surely it is far more plausible to believe that some people are more inclined one way and some people the other, and whatever they are at any one time they do not necessarily stay like that. The same people may be more 'individualist' on one day or in one context than another, which is not to say that there has been no increase in the number of enthusiasts who are generally more collectivist in their views. They are in a sense more Victorian in their ethical position, more like the Pioneers than they are to the majority of their contemporaries. For whatever reason, they prefer the collectivist ICOM model to any other. We hope that the numbers of such people will continue to grow. They are a counter to the aggressive acquisitiveness which has become endemic in modern society.

Although their numbers may well grow, their co-ops are not likely to grow so fast once they have been set up. Their outlook will make it more difficult to attract the capital necessary for rapid expansion, and, even more important than that, their ethos will be against growth. They are not, to adopt a word used by keen young businessmen of the orthodox sort, 'hungry' for large steaks, large cars, holidays in the West Indies, de luxe kitchens and saunas at their local leisure centres. If they were, they would prefer jobs in IBM or the Greater London Council to working for relatively little in the agreeable atmosphere of a SUMA. All in all, although they may survive well enough, it will not be on an expansion path and on their own they are not likely to grow fast enough to make an impression on the economy as a whole by the end of the millennium.

To do that it will have to be recognized that most people by definition are nearer the norm (for the time being) of the culture, and are more likely to be suited by a co-operative which is also nearer the norm of business organization. This suggests Mondragon more than it does ICOM.

So we come to our own conclusion in the dispute, which is simply that there should be none. There should be no either/or. People differ. Circumstances differ. Co-ops should differ. There is no single right form of constitution.

We are not asking for a cease-fire. Discussion is essential to the collective life of people who believe in co-operatives or anything else. As it continues, new sorts of resolution may be found between apparently opposing viewpoints. The debate should go on but without expecting that we will necessarily end up with a single best compromise.

But on one point alone we want to be dogmatic. The discussion needs to be carried on without the bitterness that sometimes characterizes it now. This matters so much if unity is going to co-exist with diversity that we want to ask for a seventh principle to be added to the famous six. It would be the principle of tolerance. 'Members of co-operatives with different structures should always be tolerant of each other.'

Shortage of capital

This chapter has been largely about the internal financial relationships in co-ops and not so far about the external financial relationships. This second subject is just as important as the first. A useful starting point for discussing it is the observation made by Beatrice Webb to which we have already referred. She was surely right that the shortage of capital has been a constant brake upon expansion, and too often the cause of collapse. This can be illustrated paradoxically by a grand prediction made by Mrs Webb about the future of co-operation. She wrote in 1928:

> A century hence, I am inclined to predict, school textbooks and learned treatises will give more space to consumers' co-operation, its constitution and ramifications, than to the rise and fall of political parties or the possibilities of successive Prime Ministers. For, unless I completely misinterpret the irresistible groundswell of British democracy, it is this consumers' co-operation, in its two-fold form of voluntary association of members (in what we now know as the co-operative society) and obligatory association of citizens (in the economic enterprises of national as well as Local Government) – all of them in organic connection with an equally ubiquitous organisation of the producers by hand or by brain (in trade unions and professional associations) which will constitute the greater part of the social order of a hundred years hence.[35]

She was right about the 'obligatory' associations of citizens in nationalized and municipalized industries, right too about the trade unions and professional associations, and clearly wrong about the consumer co-ops which were the apple of her eye.

Though still a powerful force in retailing and still by far the weightiest of the elements in the co-operative movement as a whole, far from moving from success to success they have faltered badly in the half-century since the prediction. If she were alive today Mrs Webb would be unlikely to renew it. Why so? Shortage of capital again – that has been one of the main reasons.

In the Webbs' time this was not an affliction of consumer co-ops, but it has become so as changes in retailing have called for more and more capital. Supermarkets have had to be built. They now dominate the grocery trades which the Pioneers entered. Sainsburys, Marks and Spencer, Tesco, Waitrose and other chain stores have been able to raise the capital. The co-operative retail societies – even the national body, Co-operative Retail Services, which has taken over so many ailing local societies, large and small, from the London Co-operative Society downwards – have not been able to raise nearly as much, with the inevitable result that *the* co-op has found it difficult to compete. The fate of Mrs Webb's prediction underlines once again the weight of the main point she made elsewhere about capital.

It is worth asking why the retail societies could not lay their hands on the capital. When the first supermarket appeared the co-ops were still riding high. If they could have afforded it they might have swept the board with large new stores, and even perhaps been first with hypermarkets when their turn came. But their co-operative structure prevented them from doing so. They could no longer generate enough capital out of their surpluses or the savings of members and yet they could not get it from outside because their constitutions forbade that.

Unless this handicap can be removed (to risk a prediction of our own so soon after bringing forth Mrs Webb's) we would not expect worker co-operatives to expand at any greater rate in the future than they have done in the last few years. In a later chapter we point to the opportunity for expansion provided by the ripeness for take-over of quite a few large companies. Ripe they may be, but from where would a co-operative get the necessary large sums of money, measured in millions, not thousands, of pounds?

To answer that question means considering the implications of the third principle. They are far-reaching. Co-ops are ordinarily bound by it to raise outside capital in the form of loans at fixed or at variable rates tied to the standard base rates of the high street banks. This has limited the amount of loans they can get. Banks and other lenders will always look at the 'gearing', that is at the relationship between shareholders' capital and the proposed borrowings. Co-ops with little shareholders' capital –

usually little because the members are seldom wealthy people and in an ICOM co-op, even if they were, they could only buy one share – are on this count at a disadvantage to begin with when they try to borrow from a commercial source. In the ordinary way banks also want security for their loans to guard themselves against a loss. They like the charge they take on buildings and other assets, or a guarantee against loss, to cover them fully. They get as near as they can to riskless lending.

Co-ops are often forced into reliance upon the little that the banks will lend because they cannot raise capital in the manner of their capitalist competitors, by offering outsiders equity shares. Co-operative enthusiasts say they *can* borrow at rates of interest which give a *proper* return to the lender. But they often cannot borrow enough, beyond the value of the security they can offer, whereas their competitors can, by means of ordinary shares. The enthusiasts have not taken account of the crucial factor of risk. They may have read Keynes; they have not read Knight.[36] The reason co-ops cannot get more capital is often that it is too risky for outsiders to provide it at fixed rates of return whereas ordinary companies can by offering, in exchange for the money, shares which entitle their holders to nothing if the business collapses but a good deal, in the form of a share of the profits, if the business succeeds. The inevitable risk taken by an individual, a pension fund or other institution in supplying new money is compensated for by the chance of a substantial gain if all goes well, and the promoters' initial hopes for the business (always optimistic as they are) are in fact realized. A capitalist company that raises money in this way has the further advantage that if it takes several years to produce a profit it does not have to pay its shareholders anything during the period but can wait until there are sufficient profits to justify declaring a dividend. Moreover the share capital never has to be repaid. But a borrower at fixed rates, whether through an ordinary loan or a debenture, not only has to pay interest but also has to repay capital irrespective of the state of the business. Borrowings can therefore force a business into bankruptcy in a way that ordinary shareholdings cannot.

It is impossible to turn around and adopt the usual capitalist method of finance by equity shares without abandoning the distinctive element of co-operatives, and opening the way for control by outside capital. Equities have obviously helped many individual businesses to get going and yet produced a state of crisis in the general capitalist system which has shown itself in inflation, unemployment and general under-investment in the economy. Our hope is that where outside control is absent, enterprises that are run by the people who work in them will in the course of time become a new model on which a more and more productive economy can be based.

Yet the difficulty has to be faced. It is as real as when Beatrice Webb wrote. Many co-operatives have failed for lack of capital; many others have been restricted to the kinds of business which need little of it and prevented from entering into expanding industries which require a high capital stake. There are as yet no co-ops making microchips or video recorders or industrial robots. Therefore, without surrendering control to outsiders, everything possible has to be done to provide co-operatives with more capital. Innovations are needed. Non-voting preference shares could bring in some extra money. Job Ownership Ltd has recommended joint ventures – a co-operative and the supplier of long-term finance would then both invest in a conventional profit-making company.[37] Barclays Bank has also introduced a new kind of Business Start Loan which could be especially appropriate for co-operatives. No interest is charged on this sort of loan which can be for amounts between £5,000 and £100,000. So in the early years, while markets are being built up and teething problems solved, the borrower pays nothing. But as the business builds up and performance improves so does the 'royalty' the bank gets on its loan, the amount being worked out with reference to the projected figures for sales. The bank, as it is put, takes 'a share in the risks without taking a share in your business'. From the co-op's point of view the royalty is better than a share in the profits and so it is from the bank's. The members of a co-op, by awarding themselves bonuses, can, if they are so minded, make sure there are no profits to declare, but it is almost inconceivable that they would want to reduce the sales on which the royalty is calculated. Further innovations of this kind will be required as more and more co-ops seek to find the capital which they need.

Conclusion

In this chapter we have described co-operatives according to the sorts of constitution they adopt. They are all businesses owned and controlled by their workers. But although that is so there are still some sharp differences between one constitution and another. Some of these we have described and, after doing so, put in our plea for more tolerance. People differ; so should the constitutions of their co-ops and the means by which they raise money if they are to overcome the first of the two main weaknesses from which co-ops suffer, their lack of capital.

4 Ways of getting started

In the last chapter we classified co-operatives in terms of the different rules they conform to. They can also be classified according to their origins.

Co-operatives begin in three main ways. They may be rescues of ailing capitalist firms. They may be conversions of successful ones. Or they may be entirely new starts. Within each type there is naturally great variation, only some of which we can capture by the examples we give.

Rescues

Far from being inspired by Robert Owen or Prince Kropotkin (a later evangelist for mutual aid), few of the workers who mount their own rescues have ever heard of a co-operative before. Theirs is a spontaneous reaction to an emergency. They would often prefer it if another businessman of the kind that they are used to would appear in place of the old. But in the absence of a saviour the only way to preserve their jobs may be to buckle to themselves and try to preserve them by their own efforts. They have to co-operate because unless they do they will be on the dole. Their only chance is to work together.

The dice are loaded against them, sometimes too much so, when it is obvious to everyone that the business is in trouble for a perfectly good and unavoidable reason. The product may be badly out-of-date and to redesign it would cost more money than anyone could possibly find; the market may have disappeared not because the product is wrong but because the competition is too strong: a key manager may have left or retired and the business cannot continue without him. If so, few workers would try to save what is evidently unsaveable. The number of bankrupt concerns turned into co-ops is small because it is so difficult to build one up upon the back of a failure.

But it is not always like that. The dice may be loaded against them but not so heavily. The previous manager may have been so extremely incompetent that to get rid of him could by itself give the business a lift. At Toptown Printers in Barnstaple in Devon – an instance we pick up in a moment – the quality of senior management was thought to be the chief trouble. They spent far too much time on the road in their posh cars without getting the orders the plant so badly needed. Save their salaries and heavy expenses, and manage the plant in the way the workers thought it should be managed and they could have a decent chance, or so they believed. At Craigton Bakery in Glasgow the management seemed to the workers to be top-heavy – with too many of them, sitting in their offices taking telephone calls, not on the shop-floor helping with production or out on the road trying to sell the pies, pancakes and crumpets which the factory could turn out in such ample supply. Get rid of the managers and do their jobs more cheaply, themselves, and they *might* be able to survive.

In other cases the local management might not be at fault at all, but be unable to stop the factory being closed by some distant head office. Or some part of the factory or one of its products might be viable even though that had not been a good enough reason for the directors to keep the whole factory open. This is the story of the Inchinnan co-op in Glasgow. There was no need to close the engineering shop just because the main tyre factory had to be closed.

One necessity is always that a person or a group of people capable of exercising leadership comes forward. Ideally, those who do would have experience of management already. But if no one about has that, the position may still not be hopeless. Shop stewards have frequently taken the initiative. They may not be the right people to turn the co-op around into a commercial success. They were not at Kirkby.[38] But they do have one substantial advantage in the confidence invested in them by the workforce.

The new venture will also have a better chance if the would-be co-operators can get the right advice from the start. They need help to get the facts which will show one way or another whether the business could work. They have to learn how to prepare business plans for banks and other financiers to consider and they need advice if they are to choose the best legal form. All this may have to be done very fast if existing customers are not to be lost to competitors, which is bound to happen unless continuous supplies can be assured. For people with no experience of management to move fast without such advice may be next to impossible. An ordinary high street banker will not give it, nor an ordinary accountant. Few of them know anything about co-ops, and what they do know may be unfavourable. Hence the importance of specialized support organizations with experience of giving help to people who would otherwise be without it. Sometimes the best advice the workers can have is not to make the attempt.

Such co-ops start from ashes. But they can have some compensating advantages. When everyone's job is at stake everyone is going to make an effort. The customary opposition to management can disappear and with it the famous two sides of industry. The outcome depends upon whether the workers can pull together sufficiently and bring forth enough ability to get through the crisis.

The early history often runs to a pattern. Wages may be reduced, quite voluntarily; indeed, the members sometimes work for nothing for a period of weeks or even months in order to secure orders and build up some working capital. They may lengthen their hours to include weekends and late nights. They may put on one side demarcations between one job and another which have been studiously upheld for many years as part of the custom of the trade. The fitter does the operator's job; the accountant turns to in the factory; the lorry driver comes in to lend an extra hand before loading starts to make sure that an order is delivered on time; the machinist repairs the building; the manager gets his hands dirty. In such circumstances people are often surprised, and pleased, that they can do things they did not do before when their jobs were specialized into a conventional division of labour.

They may be able to make. Can they sell? It is a question not just for the marketing manager, if they are lucky enough to have one, but for everyone. Each worker with useful outside contacts or any skill in selling needs to be put on to that for at least some of the time. Whatever else happens, someone has to go around to the normal suppliers of material and try to reassure them that bills will be paid and that it is safe to give credit. They must also reassure their normal customers that quality, price and delivery time will all be satisfactory. Many ordinary companies are suspicious of co-operatives. They have to be persuaded otherwise. The sense of a united labour force can in itself be a powerful argument.

The exertion of such a collective effort, in such marked contrast to the customary division of labour and responsibility, often produces a strong feeling of *camaraderie*. The evidence from all over Europe is the same. Labour disputes lessen. Absenteeism is reduced. Accidents become less frequent. The equipment is better maintained.

These are generalizations. To give an idea of how a rescue can occur we describe a particular new concern which arose out of a collapse but which is different from the Inchinnan co-operative which featured in Chapter 1. Toptown Printers of Barnstaple is as idiosyncratic as any other and it no longer ranks as a co-operative which can subscribe to all the six principles, especially the one about openness of membership. But it is of interest as showing how the common crisis can be overcome and also how an enterprise which starts off as a co-operative, in spirit if not in legal form, can easily move towards something more orthodox.

Under a different name the company from which the co-op emerged moved from London to North Devon for the sake of the development grants it could attract from the Government. Since not all the former employees wanted to move, new people had to be recruited from all over the country, not just from Devon. Peter Smith and Charlie Maynard – almost needless to say, everyone in the co-op is called by his or her first name, this being one of the marks of a co-op – joined the new company early on, Peter from the Treasurer's department of a local council, Charlie from the Medway towns. It kept going for five years until the receiver was called in. In November 1972 he decided he could not sell the business as a going concern. In Christmas week all the staff were given redundancy notices.

As we have already said, Peter and Charlie decided that the top management was the main cause of their troubles. The Chairman was so seldom in the works that Peter had as a rule to make an appointment a week ahead to see him on a Friday afternoon, always on the same subject, the worsening picture shown by the accounts. They both thought – in this being joined by others – that they could certainly do better. They only had to do the opposite of what had previously been done. A particular motive was that Charlie and many of the others had moved to Barnstaple for the sake of the job and bought houses on mortgage. If they lost their jobs – and there was no other sizeable printer in Barnstaple to take them on, otherwise they might not have taken the course they did – they could lose their houses as well. Their wives were therefore a strong and anxious supporters' club from the beginning. Over Christmas Peter and Charlie decided to carry on. They formed an inner group to prepare a plan.

The first decision was to go small. They picked from the sixty people in the workforce at the time of the closure a few more to make up a complement of seven from the shop-floor and three from the office. They chose (a) good craftsmen or people skilled at one or the other part of the office work, (b) hard workers who could be relied upon to put in eight hours' work in an eight-hour day and do overtime at nights and weekends without, at the beginning, being paid for it, (c) people who would not insist on upholding any of the demarcation distinctions which they all knew had kept their costs higher than they should have been, the rule being that every man or woman was going to be able to do everyone else's job when called upon, and (d) people who could work on their own without supervision – this because they wanted to do without the expense of paying a manager.

Their first estimate of the capital they would need on this basis was £16,500. Nine of the group took out second mortgages which brought in £13,000 and Barclays advanced a loan of £3,500 fully secured on the deeds of the house owned by Nancy, an older colleague who had worked with Peter in the office and who, because she was older, had already repaid the whole of her main mortgage. This sum they used very sparingly, acquiring everything they could on hire-purchase instead of by outright purchase. They rented much smaller premises, and instead of bidding for the machines offered by the liquidator – the prices were too high – they bought three new machines which entitled them to government grants. They got possession of these for a 25 per cent deposit. They did not buy a van but used their own cars for deliveries. While still not paid, still on the dole, they also painted the new building and got their first orders. Some of the men went away to get further training so that between them they could muster a wider range of skills. The planning and preparation took five months.

Everyone worked full out from the moment they opened for custom. They attributed this not just to the wish to save their jobs but to the risk they had taken in investing their own borrowed money in the business. Although they remained members of their trade unions, and have continued to do so, they initially cut wages by half and everyone got the same, in the office or out.

It was touch and go to begin with. They could not get more than a £1,500 overdraft from the bank on top of the loan and no credit from anyone else. They were thought of as the survivors of a company which had crashed and so was liable to crash again. They had to pay cash for everything until three months after the relaunch. Then one paper supplier said that they could go onto account. Others followed.

There was a problem too about the manager. The members did not want to have one and Charlie, who was the natural manager and in practice did the job without the title, did not want to be known as one either. No one wanted anyone about even with the name of their old boss. But this did not suit customers. When they telephoned they wanted to speak to someone with the name. Also, it was not efficient for each man to do the job he chose for himself, which was what happened when they started. At least to some extent people had to be told what to do. They all recognized as well that they were spending too much time on talk, trying to arrive at agreement on what could be quite trivial questions. So even though he nearly always succeeded in spending two thirds of his time on the printing which he liked doing best, Charlie had to take on more responsibility. All major decisions continued to be taken by the entire workforce over their sandwich-lunches.

The first year was the worst. Their wives became even more nervous than they were themselves that they would lose houses as well as jobs. But gradually the outlook improved, until by 1982 they had many youngsters as apprentices and were on the way to restoring the labour force to the size it was before 1972. But the initial shareholders have remained the same. They did not see why people who joined them later when they were set for success and the risk had gone out of it should become shareholders just like the founders. The members are therefore employing non-members, if at higher rates of pay than themselves.

As for Charlie and his initial group of colleagues, they are as highly motivated as ever. Charlie summed up the case for the new regime: 'I get a lot of satisfaction going out into the workshop of a morning and seeing all these machines and saying to myself, "they're mine, not someone else's".' Toptown has now leased a purpose-built building of its own and pays union rates or better. Early in 1982 it installed £100,000 worth of new machinery, with a further £90,000 worth to come in the following eighteen months.

The challenges to other phoenix co-operatives have been similar. The redundancy notices were if anything even more of a shock when they were handed out to employees of the Craigton Bakery in Glasgow. An additional twist was given to the occasion in the way it was referred to, as the dread day 'when the letter from England came'. The bakery had been owned by Lyons, in England. It was, as in many places elsewhere, the engineering workers who decided to put up a fight. They were able to get help, of a kind not available in Barnstaple, from the Scottish Co-operatives Development Committee, a body to which we will return in the next chapter. The SCDC sent in a general manager for the first six months.

Even so it was very tough going – 'sheer hell', in the words to us of Bob Richardson, shop steward both before and after the co-op was established. No one took any wages at all for the first five weeks or received any unemployment benefit. They often found themselves still working at midnight, sticking labels on to packs of pies and cakes, after having started work at six in the morning. 'We would sing or laugh hysterically sometimes.' After a year they were still struggling. Some people objected to the long hours they had to work without extra pay for overtime, but they were always told by their fellow-workers that if they did not like it they could leave. Despite everything, morale remained high, with everyone – even the star roundsman and salesman upon whose efforts everything else depended – being prepared to change his job to finish off a batch and get it packed up ready for delivery on one of the busy days of the week. Property in a job had given way to a sense of property in the concern.

The Randolph Leisurewear co-operative at Buckhaven in Fife is another which in similar circumstances has been helped out by SCDC. In this case SCDC staff came to the view early on that this small industrial clothing factory, despite being closed down by the group to which it belonged, had a particularly strong asset in its workforce. They were highly skilled, produced top-quality clothing and had a production manager whom the workers respected and who respected them. He was prepared to stay on as the co-operative's manager. The main lack was of anyone left on the staff with experience of marketing. SCDC, however, was able to find a new member of staff for them who eventually became sales manager.

When the co-op was formed in February 1981 each of the twenty-three members made it a loan of £100 and agreed to work without wages to start with in order to build up working capital. They hoped that they would be allowed to draw unemployment benefit while they were investing their 'sweat equity'. But appeals to the Secretary of State for Scotland and the Chancellor of the Exchequer proved fruitless. They had to do without the dole. Nevertheless, they scraped through the critical first period. A Glasgow building contractor saw a programme about them on television and when he made enquiries was sufficiently impressed not just by their spirit but by the high quality of their product and their competitive prices to place a large order with them for overalls. The police and local authorities followed, and then in the summer of 1981 came an export contract worth £3·6 million from a large Swedish contractor. As a result they have invested even more heavily in new machinery than Toptown did.

Co-operatives like these two Scottish ones are often nearer the individualist than the collectivist end of the spectrum. The workers put so much into it at the start, in sweat equity and in money, that they consider they have a right to share in the proceeds if hard work and good fortune keep them going. Sometimes the individualism goes so far that the initial group who went through the early struggles, as at Toptown, see no reason for allowing later arrivals to share in their hard-won success. The conversions from capitalist companies, to which we now come, are different. Although started by individual entrepreneurs they have more readily taken to the collectivist form. From several of them individual ownership of shares by employees has been eliminated.

Conversions

The first in chronological terms of the conversions which have lasted was John Lewis. It was established as a Partnership in 1929 by the owner of a business, in this case John Spedan Lewis, who made over his shares to the workforce or partners as they became known. Its main idiosyncrasy in this context is its size. The Partnership employs some 27,000 people – more than the whole complex of Mondragon co-operatives and almost as many as another near-co-operative which has recently been created, the National Freight Corporation. The John Lewis Partnership has 20 large department stores and 75 Waitrose supermarkets. The total capital employed in the business is some £300 million.

The Partnership certainly adheres to one of the conditions underlying the one-person, one-vote principle. There are no outside shareholders with votes. Spedan Lewis thought it was wrong that there should be any from the moment he noticed at the beginning of the century that the income which he and other members of his family drew from the business was a lot more than the whole of the pay sheet for the people who made up the business. He therefore decided that all the assets of the business should be 'owned' by employees, or at any rate held in trust for them, and the profits re-invested in the rapid expansion of both department stores and supermarkets or in various leisure amenities for the staff. The residual profits were originally distributed among the employees in the form of saleable, non-voting shares; nowadays they are distributed in cash in proportion to pay.

But though going so far Mr Lewis did not completely 'hand over' his business to his employees. He devised a constitution made up of almost as many checks and balances as that of the USA. It left a good deal of power in the hands of Mr Lewis and the man (it was then even more unthinkable that it should be a woman than that a prime minister should be) he chose to be his successor as chairman, and so on to other chairmen.

The Chairman carries weight in each of the formal bodies Lewis established – and there is a great deal of formality in the whole affair. He has a say in the composition of the Central Council, the main body elected by the individual employees which is at the heart of the constitution and which has taken on more and more responsibility as the years have gone by. Of its 130 or so members the Chairman can appoint up to a fifth but in practice appoints fewer. The Central Council elects five members of the Central Board, which acts as the board of directors, while the Chairman appoints five in addition to himself and the Deputy Chairman. The third influential body is the Trust Company which owns the equity of the holding company. Forty of the Trust Company's shares are held by the Chairman and sixty by the other Trustees who are elected annually by the Central Council. Provided it has a two-thirds majority, the Central Council can actuate the Trustees' shares.

How does it work? As usual, the practice counts more than the letter of the constitution and the practice can perhaps best be judged by reference to the objectives which underlie it. In the words of Sir Bernard Miller, who succeeded Spedan Lewis as chairman, 'The Partnership is based on the conviction that happiness will be promoted by the fairer sharing of gain, knowledge and power in the organisation in which a person works.'[39] The authors of the independent study which Miller was introducing concluded that gain had been more fairly shared – profits were distributed between all employees rather than to shareholders. Knowledge has also become more generally available. Great efforts have been made by the management to communicate with the Partners and to give them as much information about the business as they can absorb. Discussion is also encouraged in and out of the numerous *Chronicles* and *Gazettes* which are published within the group.

But the sharing of power had (according to the investigators) not got so far. The company continued to be paternalistic. This was not in any ultimate sense required by the constitution. The Central Council have the power, if they like to use it, to declare that the Chairman is no longer fit to hold that office, without giving any reasons for their decision. In these circumstances the elected Trustees acquire the full voting power of their shares and can dismiss the Chairman. That it has not happened must be due partly to the continued growth of the business, producing financial and other benefits for the people in it, so that the Chairman has the confidence of the Council. Another reason is the preference given in the elections to lower and middle management rather than the rank and file. 'They have so far proved impervious to appeals from me and many others to elect more of themselves and through the Branch Councils and Central Council have rejected suggestions for changes in the electoral arrangement that would either limit their choice or tilt the scales in favour of rank and file candidates.'[40] This being so, the ensconced junior and middle management is not likely to challenge senior management to the limit. This is not to say that Partnership is a fiction – far from it. The Industrial Common Ownership Act of 1976 defined a co-operative enterprise less stringently than we did in the last chapter as a 'body controlled by a majority of the people working for it whose income was applied for the benefit of its members'. John Lewis certainly conforms to the second of those conditions and has gone a great deal further than other large businesses towards meeting the first requirement.

After John Lewis the next largest and next most famous conversion is Scott Bader, or the Scott Bader Commonwealth to give it the name it adopted after it became a co-operative. The company was first set up by Ernest Bader, a Swiss-born businessman who settled in England and became the sole UK agent for a new product made in his home country, celluloid. By 1951 it had become a leading manufacturer of polyester resins and other intermediate chemical products in a model factory at Wollaston in Northamptonshire.

Mr Bader was a natural autocrat, a type presumably as common in Switzerland as in Britain, and more unusually also an earnest Quaker who did not like what he saw in the mirror. He said he started his Commonwealth to curb his authoritarian nature. Persuaded by George Goyder[41] and others to give his company to his workers, even when he had done so he found it galling when the unchallenged power that had once been his was in fact challenged. 'He was always to see himself as the parent both of the Commonwealth and of his people; he was to be the guide, the teacher, the expert (or expert provider), the disciplinarian, the ideas man.'[42]

But he did set up the new structure, if rather gingerly at first, remaining chairman of the Community Council, in effect the board of the holding company, until his son, Godric, took over from him in 1966. The Commonwealth was established as a charitable trust in 1951 on the strength of a gift of 90 per cent of the shares in the company which he and his family made. The other 10 per cent, with 50 per cent of the voting rights and almost all the power, was held back. All eligible employees were entitled to apply for membership of the Commonwealth, with the right to elect representatives. Gradually, with Mr Bader fighting most of the way to prevent it, the Commonwealth obtained more of the real power. Eventually in 1963 that last 10 per cent of the shares and the special rights that went with them were given up.

In straight commercial terms Scott Bader had been a successful company and was then a successful co-operative. Between 1953 and 1976 sales increased more than twenty times, and they have gone on growing. The Scott Bader Commonwealth was the power behind ICOM when it was first formed and has continued to be one of its chief financial supporters. Most of the other converted co-operatives – several of them formed under the influence of Scott Bader – have likewise been successful in commercial terms, particularly Bewley's Cafes in Dublin and Airflow Developments in High Wycombe which employs over 200 people making extractor fans and the like. Another conversion which has yet to prove itself was helped to get going by JOL. Bourlet

Frames Ltd is, as a Job Ownership Company, the successor to a company of picture framers which started life in the first half of the nineteenth century. It was acquired by the auctioneers, Sotheby's, in the early 1970s, then sold by them to the co-operative for a nominal £1 on condition that the workers raised the finance to keep it going, which they did.

We said that many co-operatives formed out of conversions lean more to the collective than to the individual form of membership. This is partly because the owner or owners who give the company away (or sell it) to a co-operative want to ensure that its capital base is not eroded, and fear that allowing individual workers rights over their shares could lead to that result. It seems safer to transfer the formerly paternalist power to a collective confined in such a way that it cannot dispose of the capital. Such a restriction is more sensible for a concern already well-capitalized than for one which is just being launched and which needs to persuade the members themselves to put up as much capital as possible. At all events, there is no denying the commercial success of many of the co-operatives which originate in conversions. There should be scope for increasing their number in the future, by persuading owners who have built up companies and want to retire to give them or sell them to their own workers rather than to an outside concern. This should generally be easier when there is a single owner and he or she has no heir.

Once again, the experience of Mondragon is to the point. Until recently conversions were not in favour. In the early days the Ulgor, Arrasate, Funcor and San Jose co-operatives all started as conversions. In the 1960s the issue did not come up as industry was booming generally, and Mondragon with it. A few years ago conversions found some favour again, subject to some tough conditions being satisfied. This was not so difficult in two out of three conversions when the Banco de Bilbao as the owner transferred the net assets to the successor co-op for nothing and paid for substantial redundancies before the transfer. In general the Caja insists that before a co-op is formed by way of a conversion 'a full study of the existing and potential state of the business should be made, with a favourable conclusion; a strong minority, including some shopfloor leaders and some of the managerial staff should be in favour; the unions should offer no formal opposition; the workers who remain should be prepared to put up a significant capital stake; the former owners should be willing to support the conversion'.[43]

New starts

In this category come all the businesses which were started as co-operatives from the beginning. They vary in their dates of origin, in the industries they form part of, in the parts of the country they have been set up in, above all in the kinds of people who form them. They include a few old CPF co-operatives established in the last century and many that although still only a few years old would be recognized as having something in common with them. Manchester Cold Rollers is, for example, a JOL company which is in manufacturing, making assembly-line systems for metal rolling. All of the founder members were graduate engineers who between them designed a machine which could sell at about 60 per cent of the market price of competitive products.

They prepared themselves by intensive training, with one member taking a new business course at Manchester Business School. Their proposal won a £7,000 prize as joint winner of the Granada TV 'Co-operate' competition and a £5,000 prize as a winner of BBC Nationwide's 'Enterprise 82' new business competition. Two youngsters came as apprentices from a Youth Opportunities Scheme and two other workers joined after 4–6 months. Having served the probationary period one worker became a full member and one apprentice will soon become one.

According to Stephen Cadney, the prime mover in the venture, the salary structure is a flattened version of that in a conventional company. The three remaining full members (one of the founders has left) are paid the same wage, £7,000 per annum, and they all 'feel the same motivation as if it was their own private business. We all work harder, we work late and sometimes do a six-day week. We don't pay ourselves overtime.' Recently the necessity to raise outside capital has made those who previously had not felt strongly about co-operatives realize the danger of having outside shareholders. The new shareholders, who are from out-side the company, have given options on their shares to the members of the co-op so that all shares can be held internally once the company can afford it.

Most of the new-start co-operatives are of recent origin, this because the general rate of expansion has been so rapid. Amongst them Manchester Cold Rollers is somewhat unusual, although by no means unique, as a manufacturer. Most of the new co-ops are in services and in other industries besides manufacturing. In this way they are generally like new firms of all kinds, which have not been to the fore in manufacturing at a time of rapid decline in Britain's manufacturing base.

Many of the newly established co-operatives have been of a kind which did not require large investments and were small enough to be able to manage without any elaborate management structure. The Otley Woodwind Co-op in Yorkshire could get by on little capital and still find a market in repairing and converting woodwind instruments.[44] So could the Bristol Musicians Co-op, whose fifteen members came together to promote alternative music; or Psychological Therapy Services, a group of five clinical psychologists in South London who at moderate charges provide their professional skills to community groups and to individuals; or the Northumbrian Energy Workshop which sets up windmills for customers and advises on renewable energy systems; or the Metro Books Co-operative, a community bookshop with seven members in Bury in Lancashire, which is itself a member of the Federation of Radical Booksellers with some forty bookshops throughout the country. The bookshops go with a range of publishers. *Spare Rib*, the women's magazine, is written by a 'collective of women for women', and the Writers and Readers Publishing Co-operative has also been highly successful, as has the Aberdeen People's Press.

The most distinctive characteristic of a new co-op is just that, by its very nature, it is a group affair. Most new firms of an orthodox kind are launched by an individual with an idea about a service or product that he can sell. He (or more rarely she) takes the initiative in collecting the right people around him. Co-ops usually need a prime mover as much as an ordinary business but not someone who wants to own the business so much as share its ownership and management with others.

How then *do* the co-operators come together? Rescue and conversion co-ops have the people on the spot already. Not so new co-ops, or not necessarily so. It can be said, as one generalization, that the initial group often have some other bond besides their willingness to join a co-operative business, and indeed that it is frequently enough this other bond which makes them consider forming a co-operative in the first place. We will give just a few examples.

All over the country women who know each other anyway have set up their own co-operatives. A co-operative manner of working, without strongly marked hierarchies, is often more attractive than it would be to an otherwise similar group of men. Women also know about the special problems they have, especially if they have young children to look after, in finding crèches or the like, in the absence of flexible hours which fit in with their domestic life, and in the discrimination they suffer from just because they are women. If they set up their own co-operative they can, as long as they can become properly commercial, arrange their affairs so that these problems are not so acute as they often are.

An example, in a traditional women's trade, is the Kennington Office Cleaners Co-operative. The initial common bond was that the founders mostly belonged to a mothers and toddlers group set up by a community worker at Lady Margaret Hall Settlement in Kennington, in South London. Many of then had been, or were, part-time office cleaners, and dissatisfied with it, disliking their supervisors, the poor pay and the lack of decent equipment and materials. Discussing how it *might* be, they decided to try and employ themselves and registered their co-op as a Friendly Society.

That far was easy. Much less so was getting cleaning contracts, even though they were near Central London and the City. Firms were suspicious of them, first because they were new, and secondly because they were a co-operative. 'If there are no supervisors,' they would be asked, 'how do you make sure the job's done properly?' They could not even get a contract from their local authority. Nothing went right for the first nine months until they won their first contract. But when they got one, others followed. Their reputation grew until at the time of going to press the co-op had twenty-two working members with hours ranging from six to fifteen a week. The success at Kennington has encouraged other women to follow and Clydeclean Cleaners Co-operative has been set up in Glasgow, Hardwork Cleaners Co-operative in Newcastle and Orton Friendly Cleaners Co-operative in Peterborough. Other networks of women's co-ops like the Bargoed Blouse Co-operative in Wales, Louise Argyle Limited at Hebburn and Ragged Robin in Lampeter[45] have likewise grown up in another traditional female industry, textiles.

Another bond is the religious one. Christian beliefs were behind many co-ops started in the last century and inspired Ernest Bader and others in this. More recently, Christianity has been joined by Buddhism. Nine co-operatives have been formed by the Friends of the Western Buddhist Order – the Right Livelihood Co-operatives which try, as they describe it, to combine the ideal of right livelihood with the radical co-operative tradition which began with Robert Owen. The four principles which guide these co-operatives are:

1 *Ethics*. No work should be done which harms, exploits or deceives any living being.

2 *Responsibility*. Everyone within the Co-operative should be prepared to – and be free to – take full responsibility for their own part in the work and for the overall policy of the business.

3 *Commitment*. Everyone in the Co-operative should be committed to the ideals of personal development and to actively pursuing them in their working lives and relationships.

4 *Generosity*. The work done should serve some wider purpose either in itself or from the profits made: the workers should, through their work, be contributing to the establishment of the conditions under which many more people can grow.[46]

Of the nine co-operatives of this sort started in the last few years, employing in all some 115 people, most have mixed businesses. The Rainbow Co-operative in Croydon runs a wholefood shop, a vegetarian restaurant and a building and decorating concern, and produces films and video tapes. The Pure Land Co-operative in Bethnal Green is in those same four businesses, plus photo-typesetting and litho printing.

Conclusion

In this chapter we have divided co-ops into three types as far as their origins are concerned. This was partly in order to throw light on what their needs are. The co-operatives formed from conversions are in several respects the best-off. They often have adequate capital and adequate management. Both these advantages are so substantial that pride of place in national government policy should (as it seems to us) be given to the encouragement of conversions. Such conversions, or co-operative companies if that were the name preferred, can be particularly valuable as a means of support for other co-ops. Scott Bader has done this for all the members of ICOM.

Co-ops in the other two categories are more often short of capital and management. But all three kinds have another need as well which can be broadly defined as sophisticated information and advice. The phoenix co-ops like Inchinnan need advice about where they might be able to raise capital and get skilled managers. So do the new starts like the Kennington Cleaners, which can also benefit greatly from federating with other co-ops in the same line of business. The members of the Kennington co-op, for instance, learnt a great deal from a national conference for all cleaning co-ops which the Mutual Aid Centre helped to finance. The conversion co-ops need advice about the best constitutions and the best ways, in law, in which conversions can be brought about. Indeed, all may need guidance about constitution-making and, more fundamentally, about the different means by which members can be given a real share in management in a way which enhances rather than impedes efficiency. They are usually small, and though that is on balance an advantage they also have a special need to federate in order to compete with larger firms which can afford more specialists on their own staffs. All this brings us to the subject of the next chapter, which is about the extent to which information and other aid does pass from one concern to another. This sort of co-operation does not just happen; it has to be organized.

5 Co-operation between co-operatives

We have now completed the first half of this book. It has been devoted largely to diagnosis. Worker co-operatives have been prominent at two previous periods in British history, in the middle of the last century under the influence of Robert Owen and the Christian Socialists and then, briefly, after the First World War under the influence of the Guild Socialists. The half-century from the early 1920s to the early 1970s was a long-drawn-out and low period. Such worker co-ops as there were kept going only precariously and in small numbers. The drive for stronger trade unions and with that the drive for orthodox public ownership under the direction of the state dominated the energies of organized workers to such an extent that co-operatives were put in the discard. During that period the future of socialism seemed to lie with state-management rather than with the self-management we ourselves are advocating.

But self-management has again emerged into prominence in the last decade, and is still on an accelerating growth path. More worker co-operatives were formed in the first quarter of 1983 than in the first three quarters of the twentieth century. Yet it would be no service to the co-ops to pretend that they have no weaknesses. They clearly do. Obviously we do not share the pessimism of Beatrice Webb or we would not be writing this book. But we think that the reasons she gave for her pessimism – though they did not justify her sweeping conclusion – were perfectly sound. Co-ops continue to suffer from the two shortages, in capital and management, which she identified. Their promise will be fulfilled only if these weaknesses can be overcome or moderated.

So much for the diagnosis – which varies a bit, as we have

just seen, according to the manner in which the co-op originated. The main issue for the rest of this book is about the steps which could be taken to overcome or minimize the defects – about capital and management of course and also about the need for more mutual aid which was picked out at the end of the last chapter. We shall start with the help which co-operatives can give to each other.

The gospel on what should be done is straightforward enough. The sixth ICA principle in its full formulation spelt it out more fully than we did earlier. 'All co-operative organisations, in order to best serve the interests of their members and their communities, should actively co-operate in every practical way with other co-operatives at local, national and international levels.'[47] The question is how far worker co-operatives have lived up to the precept, not just by supporting each other (this being the main intent of the sixth principle) but by creating organizations which will serve them all.

The retail societies, for instance, were drawn together not so much by the ethic embodied in the sixth principle, though that has helped, as by sheer commercial necessity. In their heyday there was a society for almost every district in the country. Organized on this simple territorial basis though they were, they did sometimes compete, and when they operated in the same street their enmity was mutual. But by and large they did not compete and so could more readily co-operate with each other for their mutual benefit. Many of them were small. To remain so and yet to compete with some of the larger privately owned stores which were in the same line of business they had to embrace some of the advantages of the large scale without forfeiting the advantages of smallness. This is a fundamental proposition for all co-operatives, not just consumer societies. To succeed (in this, indeed, like all organizations, whether co-operative or not) they have to blend in a distinctive way the two opposite economies of scale, the small and the large together.

The retail societies recognized that long ago. To begin with, in the astonishing burst of energy which occurred at Rochdale, not only did the Pioneers start the manufacturing society which, as we have said, demonstrated once again that nothing fails like success; they also made their Equitable Society the chief repository of working-class savings in their area. They established a co-operative corn mill as the first joint venture with other societies to grind corn for all of them. They set up the Rochdale Equitable Provident Sick and Burial Society, the Rochdale Co-operative Card Manufacturing Society, a Co-operative Building Society and the Co-operative Insurance Company (which later became the present Co-operative Insurance Society).[48] The Pioneers then set out to buy for other co-ops and to become the general wholesaler for other societies. In the 1850s they were set to become a general co-operative support body with working-class savings to draw on, the Mondragon of their day – not just the first viable consumer co-operative but very much the first in the world to create a viable network in which every co-operative supported every other.

As it turned out, the Pioneers decided that a general wholesaler owing allegiance not just to them but to societies in other places as well would do better for the growing movement than they could. So in 1863, when the main Rochdale Society had just topped 4,000 members, they took the leading part in establishing the Co-operative Wholesale Society. It was not easy to get agreement. Huddersfield and Halifax had different tastes in butter. How would one wholesale buyer satisfy them both and still buy cheaper in bulk? But at a crucial conference in Manchester, Huddersfield and Halifax and the others came to agreement. From that emerged common buying and common manufacturing in CWS (or Scottish CWS) factories as well as the Co operative Bank and eventually the Co-operative Union. The CWS has in this century been the force behind Co-operative Retail Services which has rescued from failure so many local societies, even if it has sometimes done so at the expense of local democracy.

For worker co-operatives there is no equivalent to the CWS or, for that matter, to the Central Council for Agricultural and Horticultural Co-operation which we refer to in the next chapter. This is true to some extent of other countries as well. 'While agricultural, consumer and savings co-operatives have developed powerful secondary organisations in many countries, this has not generally been the case with industrial co-operatives.'[49] But there are exceptions and it is from these that we in Britain should be able to learn, particularly from countries which are also in

the Common Market if we include Spain as at any rate a prospective member. Italy and France, as well as Spain, have the
strongest worker co-operatives in Western Europe and – it can
hardly be a coincidence – the strongest support organizations as
well.

Europe ahead

Italy has many more worker co-operatives – over 5,000 of them
– than any other Common Market country and indeed more
than the rest of Western Europe put together. The explanation
lies in Italian history.[50] In the 1880s there was much the same
development of producer co-ops as in Britain and France. The
first co-operative federation was formed in 1886, which became
the Lega Nazionale delle Co-operative e Mutue, known for short
as the Lega. Compared to Britain the difference is that the growth
was uninterrupted, especially in the form of labour-only co-ops
which gained contracts for the supply of labour without having
to find the capital to go with it, for instance in civil engineering,
or in providing all the staff for a port or even a railway, with the
port or the railway itself and its equipment being owned by an
authority which contracted with the co-op. (A labour-only co-
op could, likewise, be hired by a local authority in Britain to
maintain council blocks or run the refuse system but using the
council's vehicles and plant.) By 1921 there were 3,000 labour-
only co-operatives in existence in Italy; most of them were
carrying out large and small contracts in the public sector for
the construction of roads, bridges, harbours and other public
works. As organizations they were, in a new form, made up of
the kind of independent artisans who had for centuries been the
backbone of the Italian building industry. They were always
able to exert a good deal of political influence.

Until 1919 the Lega was the national organization. After that,
following the Russian Revolution, it became more overtly political, forming direct links with the Italian Socialist Party. This
led to a breakaway of a separate Catholic grouping, the Confederazione Co-operative Italiane. When the Italian communists in
their turn split from the socialists the Lega remained with the
communists. But eventually, after 1945, the socialists re-asserted

themselves and a third republican and social democrat federation, the Associazione Generale delle Co-operative Italiane, was set up.

Individually, and sometimes collectively, the influence of these federations has, except during the Mussolini period, been almost continuously effective, so much so that article 45 of the new national constitution adopted after the Second World War guaranteed that 'the state would assist the development of co-operatives'. To give effect to this, interest on members' capital was made exempt from tax, co-operatives were made eligible for low-interest government loans and both provincial and local authorities were permitted to give special preference to them.

The political divisions between the three federations are, if a disadvantage, not a total one. Since the war there has always been a government in power with links to one or other of the federations. They also have a comprehensive sweep. Each federation includes all types of co-operative – agricultural, consumer, worker, credit. Thus, in the one region of Emilia Romagna there were recently inside the Lega alone 275 consumer co-ops, 475 worker co-ops, 677 in agriculture, 357 in housing, 46 in transport, 9 in fisheries and 241 of mixed types.[51] The growth in service co-operatives – taxis, driving schools, catering, portering, newspaper distribution, social and professional services – has been rapid in this region as elsewhere in Italy. The advent of management consultancy co-operatives which are prepared to advise other co-operatives as well as public and private bodies of many different sorts is another new phenomenon.

Since co-operatives of all types are inside each head organization, inter-co-operative arrangements are easy to make. They are encouraged to buy and sell to one another, to buy in common, to form consortia to gain export orders, to support research and development conducted on behalf of several co-operatives at once, to advertise together, and above all to pay for the staff at national and regional offices and in the sectoral associations for building and other co-operatives. These staff are available to help any co-operative which calls upon them for aid and also take advantage of any good opportunity to rescue a capitalist firm that has gone bankrupt or is in danger of doing so.

The French movement has even deeper roots in history. The

self-governing workshops for carpenters, shoemakers and printers established in 1830 and afterwards by Louis Blanc, Fourier
and others were for a time a sensation throughout Europe. A few
years later, after the 1848 Revolution, 200 new co-operatives
were established within a period of a few weeks. The great
majority failed. But eventually a solid base was established.
More than a third of the 726 worker co-operatives existing in
1980 were founded before 1945.

The federal body of French worker co-operatives is known as
SCOP. Like the Italian federations it is itself a 'secondary' co-
operative, being made up of the worker co-operatives who belong to it and control it. SCOP is financed by a turnover levy on
worker co-ops and a grant from the Government to help it rescue
firms that would otherwise disappear. SCOP has ten regional
'unions' covering the whole of France; in the majority of them
the regional office or *délégation* can provide a full range of support
services. These are grouped in three main categories: legal support, financial support and what is called 'development support'.

The funds available for direct financial expansion are modest
and come from the 'Confederal Fund for Expansion' (Fonds
d'Expansion Confédéral), which is financed by a 1 per cent levy on
the sales of member co-operatives. In the creation and preservation of jobs the key services come from the Development
Support Division in Paris, which is a smaller version of the
Empresarial Division of Mondragon with a much larger number
of co-operatives to look after. The Paris Division has played a
part in the saving of jobs in many of the well-known companies
which have been turned into co-ops in the last decade, such as
Manuest in the furniture industry. The advance of SCOP has
been aided by several social surveys which have found that in
co-operatives workers have more sense of responsibility than in
capitalist firms, have a much greater sense of belonging, a better
working atmosphere and more freedom of expression.[52]

SCOP, if not itself a cross-sectoral federation like the Italian
ones, is helped by having a well-recognized place in the wider
co-operative movement. The Groupement National de la Co-
opération (National Co-operative League) represents all sections,
farming, consumer, fishing, housing, workers, craftsmen and the
powerful co-operative banks. Among these banks the Crédit Agri-

cole, with 60,000 employees, is said to be the second largest bank in the world. There is also an official body, the Conseil Supérieur de la Co-opération, where representatives of co-operatives and the Government meet to discuss matters of state policy. In France a patchwork of individual co-operatives and sectional groupings has to some extent given way to a single co-operative movement with the potential to exert economic and political influence on an increasing scale.

As for Spain, we have already said a good deal in passing about Mondragon, but perhaps without stressing enough the many-sidedness[53] of the support system. It is no exaggeration to say that there is a *web* of support not just between the Caja at the centre and the individual co-operatives – this is a two-way affair, with the Caja having a financial stake in the co-ops and the co-ops a financial stake in the Caja – but between the co-ops themselves and also between them and a number of other supporting organizations. They get on so well and understand each other so well in some part because every co-op has, basically, the same constitution. All this is brought out vividly in the book by Thomas and Logan, which contains the fullest account of Mondragon yet published.[54]

The book shows, for instance, how crucial the Caja is as a supplier of credit on top of the capital that has to be put in by individual members of co-ops to 'buy' the equipment they will need in their jobs. New co-ops have priority. 'In 1979 investments per person were 297,000, 150,000, 394,000, and 810,000 pesetas respectively for the old, middle-aged, young and very young co-operatives. Irrespective of the dismal cash flow position during the start-up years, the young and very young co-operatives have been given strong support in their investment programmes.' Most new co-ops are carried by the bank in their early years until they begin to make surpluses. New co-ops are watched by the Caja even more closely than old-established ones. Indeed, one of the many important functions of the Caja is to maintain statistics of performance to enable one co-op to be compared with another and co-ops generally with ordinary businesses in the Basque country and elsewhere.

Multiple links between similar co-ops are also strongly encouraged. This practice was started by Ulgor, the founding co-operative which is still the core of the whole. Ulgor began by making paraffin cookers and the British Aladdin stove and swiftly expanded from there. Its deliberate policy was to diversify. Ulgor set up Fagor to manufacture butane cookers and linked itself to Ederlan, an iron and steel foundry, and Arrasate, another co-op which moved into machine tools. Before long there was an Ularco group, as it was called. Its member co-ops did not compete among themselves. As well as selling each other semi-finished products like castings they shared in every other possible way. The policy is to launch further co-operatives of co-operatives. A second group – Biharko – was made up of five furniture co-ops all located near to each other. Of the 150 or so Mondragon co-operatives the majority are also organized into ten geographical groups, Urkida being the one for the Urda Valley, Nerbion for Bilbao, Indarko for Vizcaya Province and so on. The implication is that never, if it can be avoided, should just one co-op be set up on its own: it will have a better chance to succeed if it is organically linked with others.

This does not by any means exhaust the list of support organizations. The League for Education and Culture is one, responsible in a general way for all the Mondragon schools, colleges and polytechnics. Even a single educational hostel can play its part in the whole.[55] The hostel in question, the Colegio Menor Viteri, caters for about 350 students at any one time, half at the higher technical level and half at the middle technical level. The strategy is to select the students each year from particular communities in which new co-ops are being started so that when they return they will form a nucleus of people imbued with 'co-operative values' as well as technical skills. During 1975, for instance, 38 students came from the town of Guernica and 33 from Marquina, both located about 50 km from Mondragon. The small staff of the hostel also organize workshops and conferences in towns and villages which are near co-operatives, actual or potential. The educational network is reinforced by Ikerlan, a Research and Development co-operative which does research for all member co-ops as well as prospective ones, by Lagun-Aro, the social security co-operative, and by Eroski, the flourishing chain of consumer co-operatives.

The British case

Where does that leave Britain? Clearly we cannot expect to reach in one jump the level of organization already achieved in Italy and France, let alone Mondragon. But we can learn from their experience and at least move towards a closer network than we have got at the moment.

Our concern here is much more with worker co-ops than it is with any other sort. Nevertheless, these three countries show that it can be valuable for worker co-ops to be linked to other kinds. The Groupement National de la Co-opération in France can sometimes speak up effectively for worker co-ops because it has behind it all the other co-ops as well, including the agricultural co-ops which are in almost all countries both economically and politically the most important of all. Worker co-ops inside the Italian federations also benefit from being linked with the others. The nearest body we have in Britain to the ones in France and Italy is the Co-operative Union. Its handicap is that its exclusive political affiliations with the Labour Party are bound to put off agricultural and some other co-ops. It is the same in many other countries where worker and consumer co-ops are close to parties of the left and farming co-ops to parties of the right. Even so, the Co-operative Union is clearly the body to build on. The Union serves the consumer societies with advice on finance, law and taxation and could do more of the same kind for worker co-ops. It also has its own Co-operative College at Loughborough, an economic and research department and a publishing department – all of which could be useful.

When it comes to worker co-ops, almost whatever happens to the Co-operative Union in the future, they will certainly need their own special support body as well. Which should it be? We mentioned in Chapter 3 the four main ones there are at present without saying anything much more than where they stood on the Six Principles.

The Co-operative Productive Federation was formed at the end of the last century when the main body of the UK's co-operative movement decided to 'go consumer'. It was the federal body of the never very large number of old 'working-class' producer co-operatives which had grown up with the movement and wished to retain some sort of separate identity. At its height, in the years before the First World War, its membership may have numbered more than 100. But it went into a steady decline after 1918. By the early 1970s its member co-ops had dwindled to eleven. After an interim period of some years the CPF was absorbed by the Co-operative Union in 1980. This sequence of events may serve to illustrate a general point. A support organization in the form of a federal body which, because of lack of resources, is unable to offer much in the way of real services will eventually disappear. But for these co-ops that role has now been taken over by a much more powerful body in the Co-operative Union.

The Industrial Common Ownership Movement is the second support organization and the one to which most worker co-operatives belong – well over 600 of them at the time of going to press. Its model rules have been particularly well-used in their two main forms, first for co-operatives registering under the Industrial and Provident Societies Acts with the Registrar of Friendly Societies, and second for a common ownership company under the Companies Acts. These proved popular for new co-operatives with fewer than seven members, the minimum necessary for the other sort of registration. By the end of 1981, 40 per cent of new registrations were of co-ops with the legal form of companies.

ICOM also deals with the Government. Its greatest success, with the support of the three major political parties of the time, was in securing the passage of the Industrial Common Owner-ship Act of 1976 'to further the development of enterprises controlled by people working in them'. ICOM already had asso-ciated with it a revolving fund in the form of Industrial Common Ownership Finance (ICOF) which had been set up in 1973 with support from Scott Bader. The 1976 Act provided ICOF with an additional £250,000 which was used to supply co-ops with loan capital. Under the Act a grant of £20,000 p.a. for five years was also given to ICOM itself to enable it to set up an office and employ full-time staff. Early in 1982 it had a staff of three, with Mike Campbell as Director. ICOM has built up and services an all-party parliamentary group.

With its small staff, it is limited in what it can do to help co-ops with advice. But the staff do what they can both by themselves and by making use of volunteers. ICOM's Register of Skills lists individual members who are specialists in law, accountancy, management and other fields. Here is one example of what can be done, taken from ICOM's own Newsletter for January/February 1981:

In Berkshire a minor piece of 'rationalisation' was taking place. A very small subsidiary of a large multi-national happened to occupy a very valuable piece of real estate and the parent decided to sell the business (that is the machinery and goodwill) to a competitor and thus be able to realise its assets. The workforce was made redundant. The product, specialised components for the packaging industry, had a stable market; the former employees were sure that they would make a go of the business on their own behalf and eventually contacted ICOM. Two volunteers from our Register of Skills worked hard on behalf of the potential co-operative; consulting with the parent company, suppliers, customers, the Co-operative Development Agency, local political bodies etc. and eventually helped draw up a feasibility study for submission to ICOF. The new co-operative is now registered.

The next body is the Co-operative Development Agency. It is not representative like ICOM. Its history dates back to 1970. In that year the Co-operative Congress, the annual meeting attended by delegates from the retail societies, passed a resolution calling for such a body to be set up. In 1974, after the Labour Party had been returned to power, the Congress renewed its demand for an agency 'both to stimulate research and finance methods of restructuring existing societies on a more efficient basis.... The Labour Government should, we believe, now take steps to set up a Co-operative Development Agency to encourage rationalisation, modernisation and innovation in the co-operative sector of the economy.' The Government did as governments usually do, nothing – until, three years later, it set up the inevitable committee. The Working Group included representatives of consumer, housing, agricultural, credit and worker co-operatives. As could have been predicted, they did not agree.

All were in favour of a Co-operative Development Agency. But of what sort? The majority wanted its members to be appointed by the Secretary of State for Industry. How else could a flow of public money be assured unless it was to be given to people whom the Government appointed and could dismiss and who were accountable, therefore, to the Government which was to pass over the taxpayers' money? The minority – two of them from housing co-operatives, one from the National Federation of Credit Unions and one from ICOM – were indignant at the very idea. 'We find it difficult', they said in their minority report, 'to see how a body on which co-operative organisations are refused the right to appoint their own representatives direct can claim to speak on behalf of the movement.' They also thought, unlike the majority, that their own sectors – housing, credit, worker – should get priority over the still very large and self-sufficient consumer societies, and that the CDA should be able to provide Government-backed financial guarantees for the sort of new co-operatives they came from.

Despite the dissension, the report was followed by an Act and a CDA appointed by the Government as the majority had wanted. But when it was set up the CDA came near to following the minority report in one respect. It decided to concentrate on worker co-ops. For them it has so far provided several of the same services as ICOM, but on a larger scale because it has had more money. It has issued its own model rules and other rules too for a new kind of co-operative. The Neighbourhood Service Co-operative is modelled on the community co-operatives like the one in Eriskay we described earlier but designed for urban areas. The CDA's rules allow such a co-op to perform almost any service which a community needs and lacks. Its members can be part-time and unpaid workers as well as full-time and paid.

As well as that, CDA also deals, on behalf of co-ops, with the Government. It succeeded, for instance, in persuading the Chancellor in 1981 to amend his 1978 Finance Act to allow members of co-ops relief from income tax on money used to pay interest charges on capital they borrow. It has also given advice to local authorities and to many would-be and actual co-operators on how they should proceed. Any one of its annual reports shows how wide a coverage it has had. Here, from the 1980-1 report, are some examples of new co-operatives they advised:

> In August 1980 a clothing manufacturer in Wales announced the closure of his factory. 17 of the machinists, all members of the

Transport and General Workers, decided to carry on, as a co-operative, and approached CDA which has given as much help as it could in developing a business and marketing strategy.

A community arts centre registered as a co-operative and then sought advice from the CDA, which was that it needed a business plan as well as a cultural programme. A study was made for the centre by the Agency and a local management college.

The sole proprietor of a large antiques centre with 20 dealers as tenants, with the help of CDA turned his business into a co-operative with the 20 dealers as members.

A nursery was set up as part of a neighbourhood co-operative. CDA advised the mothers on how to deal with the local authority and how to get finance and premises.

When the Government took the decision in 1982 to extend the life of the CDA it also appointed a new Board. When Dennis Lawrence, who had been a civil servant, retired as Director his place was taken by George Jones, a businessman who was seconded from his post as a senior director of Unilever. Ralph Woolf, the Chief Executive of Scott Bader, became Chairman at the same time. Since then change has been in the air and the CDA may well become a very different affair even within the course of a year or two. It has not so far had a clear function which distinguishes it sufficiently from that of ICOM. This role it is now creating for itself.

Job Ownership is the fourth national organization, also with its own model rules. Advice has been given to many would-be co-operators including owners of businesses who are considering possible conversions. A few JOL-type co-ops have been set up, notably Manchester Cold Rollers and Bourlet Frames, and more may be in existence by the time this book is published.

These four are the principal UK organizations. There are also a number of others which serve a part of the country. The outstanding one is the Scottish Co-operatives Development Committee. It was formed in the mid-1970s by six founding bodies – the Co-operative Union, the Scottish Council of Social Service, the Scottish TUC, ICOM, ICOF and the Workers' Educational Association. In 1977 it was recognized by the Government as one of the official bodies entitled to receive funding under the Industrial Common Ownership Act. SCDC also has its model rules which are very like ICOM's except that their chosen instrument is a company limited by guarantee.

The main difference from the national organizations is that SCDC has been able to give more concentrated attention to the co-operatives coming under its wing because it has a smaller geographic area to cover, just as Wales is to have that capacity as a result of the initiative taken by the Wales TUC.[56] In 1977, when Cairns Campbell was appointed its first full-time Development Officer, there were only four worker co-ops in the whole of Scotland. By January 1982 there were 31. Many of them first sprang into existence on the strength of the support they got from SCDC, and this at every stage, from the initial feasibility study through to the formation of the co-operative, the search for key managers, and the supply of continuing advice. SCDC has always focused on the need for co-operatives to be run as efficient businesses and picked out the lack of proper managerial skills in many co-operatives as their chief weakness. In doing this it is as near the Caja as any organization in Britain established so far. The Scottish Development Agency has now agreed to an experimental scheme which should secure support for it until 1985 and to consider applications for funding for premises, equipment and working capital that come in from co-operatives backed by SCDC.

Scotland also has the Highlands and Islands Development Board, a government body which has given special support to community co-operatives of the Eriskay type. The idea was borrowed from Ireland.[57] Such a co-operative can be defined, in its Scottish context, as a multi-functional business owned and controlled by the residents of the community it serves. It raises capital from these residents and from matching funds from the HIDB and uses the money to make its community more self-sufficient. Being nearer to a consumer than a worker co-op, it has been included here because the creation of more local employment is always one of the main objectives. When a community co-operative creates new jobs in fish farming, craft marketing or tourist accommodation, the enterprises are in practice similar to worker co-ops even though the form of organization is different.

Local support bodies

The largest expansion in the last few years has not been at the national and regional levels so much as at the local. The bodies have several different names. Some are called local co-operative development agencies, some co-operative development groups, some ICOMs, some common ownership associations. By August 1982 over sixty such local groups had been formed. They also had a variety of sponsors, not always local. The Ecology Party was responsible for the group in Norwich and the Co-operative Party for the one in Oxford. But usually the initiative has been taken by a local body. In some places co-operative societies have made the first move, with the Royal Arsenal Co-operative Society having been one of the most energetic of the sponsors. In others existing worker co-operatives have taken the initial steps of calling upon each other to 'federate' at this level and to invite other local bodies to join with them. And increasingly local authorities like the Hackney Borough Council have been drawn in, as initiators or, if not that, as funders. Without financial and other support from them, motivated by their increasing concern for local employment, the groups would not have multiplied as they have. Not all local authorities have been as active as the West Midlands County Council, to take one example. It has established one CDA for the county and three more local CDAs for particular districts within it, in Coventry, the Black Country and Birmingham, and set aside £250,000 for financial support of co-operatives in the three districts. The Black Country CDA, soon after its foundation, appealed to people to come forward with ideas for new co-operatives and had 150 enquiries as a result, about 100 of which were judged worth considering seriously. There was as much interest in Coventry, where three to four new contacts were being made each day soon after the start. Some of the first proposals were for co-ops in vehicle maintenance, making concrete paving slabs, catering, building and publishing.

No one local group is quite like another. The CDA in the London borough of Brent is another example. It was started in 1980, on the initiative of Clive Grace from the local law centre, its aim being to contribute towards 'alleviating deprivation and distress in Brent'.[58] With the support of trade unionists in the local trades council and a strong local tenants federation, the first money came from an urban aid grant. The CDA soon had a staff of four: two development workers, a legal adviser and a financial adviser. Their grant is currently running at the rate of £50,000 a year, guaranteed for two years but with a possible extension for three years beyond that.

The main job of the staff is consulting and not just for worker co-ops, although these are their main concern. They are also involved with several fair-rent housing co-ops, a tenant management co-op and two community co-ops, in Kilburn and Harlesden, whose aim is to provide workshop space and advice for new businesses as well as leisure and sports facilities. Premises are, as almost everywhere, difficult to find; one of their projects is to divide a building into nursery units for four co-ops and another possible one for the conversion of a multi-storey car park into workshops. Most such car parks are failures on the part of the planners, if less spectacular than tower blocks. People avoid leaving their cars in them for fear that there will be nothing except a burnt hulk to take out in the morning. The Brent CDA may have come up with a novel form of recycling.

In their main work as consultants to worker co-ops the staff spend a great deal of time on assessing the feasibility of any new project and, if the decision is favourable, helping to raise the money for it. In the middle of 1982 two new worker co-ops had started, nine were on the way and six possible conversions of existing firms into co-ops were being worked on. One of these is for saving about sixty jobs in a GEC company, Associated Automation, which was being closed. For this they were considering a two-tier company; the workers through their company would have management control but the financiers through another company would have partnership with them which assured them a share in the profits somewhat equivalent to an equity.

The Wandsworth Enterprise Development Agency is another local group in London which has relied on urban aid finance. It was founded by the London borough of Wandsworth, Industrial Common Ownership Finance and the London Chamber of Commerce in order to provide business advice and management monitoring for common ownership enterprises in the district.

On its board it has one councillor from the majority party and another from the minority party. Penny Brookings was the General Manager and Manuela Sykes (then Chairman of ICOM) the Secretary. By the end of the first full year of operation it had helped to set up five new co-operatives – Textile Enterprises Ltd, manufacturing a range of nursery clothing; South London Bakers' Co-operative; Co-Design Ltd, a commercial art studio; Hillside Common Ownership Day Nursery, a private company converted into a workers' co-op and strongly supported by the parents; and Weslon Caricom, builders. As well as responding to approaches made to them, the staff of the Agency had defined three product areas in which they expect substantial growth – plastics processing, leisure, hobbies and sports equipment and micro-processors. They hoped to be able to entice people into establishing co-ops in these growth markets. As in Brent, the staff are primarily business consultants.

It is obvious that, whatever happens at the national level, help like that given in Brent and Wandsworth will be needed locally. People who want to start new co-operatives need somewhere local they can go to. They need advice on the spot, above all in the early stages, from those who are prepared to take trouble with very small businesses.

Most CDAs would not have got going without the backing of their own local authorities. Without money they could not employ staff and this has come out of funds for the inner cities available to some authorities under the Inner Urban Areas Act of 1978 and, more generally but more parsimoniously, by invoking the power to spend up to a 2p rate given to local authorities by Section 137 of the Local Government Act of 1972. The support of local authorities is most welcome and the hope is that it will continue. There are disadvantages, of course. Most of the authorities which have backed co-ops are Labour. If elections go against them and control of the council changes, support may be withdrawn. They are also liable to be too much under the influence of local councillors. Even so, the support of local authorities is at this stage quite vital. A further need is for local co-operative development agencies to recruit more people with business experience to act as consultants and to train more of their present staff for the same purpose.

The need to federate

The rapid growth of worker co-ops in the last few years has been reflected in an equally rapid development in the number and variety of support bodies. The ship is edging into the harbour and boats flutter up from all sides to surround it. This is to be welcomed. It is all a sign of liveliness at a very dead period for the economy in general. But we are convinced that the time has now come for the support bodies to pull themselves together into a more coherent framework.

What sort of framework? Fortunately we do not in Britain need different national bodies for the various political parties, as in Italy. The Spanish and French models are more to the point. A body comparable to SCOP would be a single national federation with a council elected by the individual co-ops belonging to it, and responsible to them. Once such a unification had been achieved the body would carry much more weight with the Government than a variety of separate organizations, appearing to be fragmented, could ever do. As the federation established itself more and more as *the* centre in the country, people wanting to start up new co-operatives, or people who had done so and wanted advice, would turn to it, as would banks, commercial companies and the press and television when they wanted an authoritative view from worker co-ops. The present impression is not so much of a movement but of a collection of bodies which spend too much time criticizing each other.

What should be the relationship of local co-operative development agencies to the proposed federation? The individual co-ops in each locality should be members of the federation and so would be represented directly on it. Votes would be cast by the individual co-ops, at national and local levels. But there could, and should, of course be a section of the national federation concerned with local federations and with individual well-wishers and at the annual congress their representatives could meet separately as well as together with others. Individual co-ops in particular industries should also be encouraged to come together into trade groupings on Mondragon lines. The relationship envisaged between the different levels and bodies is shown in Figure 2.

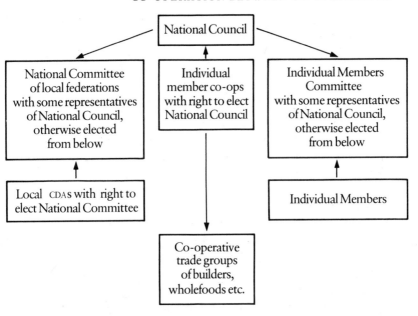

Figure 2.   Proposed Federation of Worker Co-operatives

We have now said a little about the formality of a federation but not about its functions. The most important of these by far would be to do everything possible to improve the management of co-operatives, and we will come back to that in a moment. But the new federation would have other roles as well and it may be worth at least listing them. It would:

a) act as the representative of worker co-operatives in dealings with the Government and other national bodies like the TUC and the CBI;

b) provide start-up services, including the whole range of model rules there is at present, and legal advice;

c) advise about finance for new co-ops and for expansion of existing ones;

d) encourage inter-co-operative trading;

e) build up linkages between co-operatives in the same industry or with other interests in common;

f) arrange joint tendering and contracting for home and export orders;

g) arrange joint advertising on the basis of a common logo for all worker co-ops;

- h) provide a clearing-house of information about co-ops in the UK and abroad;
- i) and take responsibility for education and training of managers and other members of co-operatives.

To our minds, the formation of such a federation, if only to act as the national voice for worker co-operatives, is quite as necessary as the TUC is for the trade-union movement or the CBI for ordinary employers and their different associations. The difficulty lies not so much in making out a case for it as in showing how to move towards it from a stage occupied at present not by one but by four different support bodies. The problem could solve itself if Britain had a government committed to the encouragement of co-ops with a powerful leverage over what happens. The mere existence of such a government might well persuade co-ops to set up a single federation to negotiate for them with ministers and civil servants.

But as things are now, can any progress be made? Could any of the four become *the* federation? The CDA should not, as long as it is financed by the taxpayer and remains as a consequence responsible to Parliament. What of the other three? ICOM has the strongest claim. Almost all the co-ops in the country are already members of it, as we have said, and at its Annual General Meeting in September 1982 some important changes were introduced into its constitution with the object of making the ICOM General Council a body more fully elected by its member co-ops. Majority control of ICOM by individuals within co-operatives was replaced by majority control by the co-operatives themselves, thereby transforming ICOM into more of a federal body than it had previously been. Local CDAs were also given a more formal role within it.

But if ICOM were installed as the all-embracing federation an orthodoxy could come with it which would not be conducive to the kind of expansion we are hoping for in this decade, with the target being more like a million members for worker co-ops than a few tens of thousands. ICOM has not been sympathetic to the Mondragon type of structure, while we are. The Basque co-ops have grown so fast and so far weathered the recession so well because they have required members to take a personal financial stake in the businesses they own, because they have seen to it that they are properly financed by the bank to compete with the best of capitalist industry, and because they have insisted on strong management responsible to the members but fully capable of exercising discipline. These are not characteristics which appeal to many ICOM members.

At the same time we recognize that the ICOM style of co-operative is fine for some people and some purposes. SUMA, described at the beginning of this book, is an admirable organization, and there are very many others like it. What we are pleading for, once again, as we did in Chapter 3, is the recognition that in this field there are horses for courses. The ICOM model suits some, Mondragon others, CDA and JOL models still others. It is a sign of health rather than the opposite that at this stage there should be different bodies with different points of view to express. But the present plurality of bodies should not preclude the setting up of one federal organization – they could co-exist with each other – as long as there was enough tolerance between them.

The 1982 report of the Co-operative Development Agency acknowledged that since its early days 'there had been a certain degree of rivalry between the Agency and the Industrial Common Ownership Movement'. It continued: 'ICOM recognised that the Agency's statutory remit required it to promote all kinds of co-operative and that it could not cease the promotion of any particular kind'. If ICOM would accept that those words should also apply to itself the way could be clear for it to become the new federation, even without a new government.

Improvement of management

Our hope is that, whether it arises from ICOM or not, a new federation would be particularly concerned with the quality of management. We have up to this point left the second major Webb criticism rather on one side. We should not do so any longer. In so far as Mrs Webb was saying that good management is impossible we certainly do not agree with her. To her this proposition was almost self-evident, at the end of the last century when so many co-ops had ended in failure. It was enough, or seemed enough, to say that *obviously* a manager, on the railways or anywhere else, could not issue orders to members of the co-op by day if in the evening they could dismiss him from office. Members could not be masters and servants at the same time.

That this dilemma, if it is one, can be resolved is shown well enough by Mondragon, and by many British co-ops as well. Beatrice Webb almost seemed to be imagining that the members would get together on any evening and discipline a manager who tried to discipline them. This could easily lead to disaster – she was right about that. Discipline, for the most part freely accepted as essential for the preservation of members' jobs, is as much a necessity in a co-operative as in any other sort of business. Managers must have the power to impose discipline, including the power to sack individual members of the co-op who are not pulling their weight. But of course it is a power delegated to them by the members. The best way in which this can be done is to provide that the general manager or managing director should not be elected directly but appointed by the board of directors who are elected not by the outside shareholders but by the inside shareholders. Once appointed for a period of years with a contract of service like that in other businesses, the manager should be left free to get on with the job under the board which is responsible for policy.

To say this (if that were all there was to it) might suggest that the manager's job in a co-op is no different from that anywhere else. This is not so. That the workers to whom he gives orders are the owners of the business and have the ultimate power to get rid of him does make a difference, and is intended to. It means that he has always to carry the worker-members with him. He has to manage by general consent. Beatrice Webb saw that this was true of co-ops and concluded that therefore they must fail. At the time when she was writing, in the 1890s, she may well have been right. Relationships at work were very different from what they have since become. Many jobs were physically very strenuous, even degrading. Men and women were driven to do them by bosses more like Gradgrind than Owen. Since then some of the grind has been taken out of most work and in all businesses managers and owners have lost much of the unchallengeable authority they once had. Their right to power is questioned; most tellingly of all, they are more apt to question it themselves, in their own minds. Consequently, managers in all sorts of businesses have to a much greater extent than they did to manage by consent. They have at least to try and carry their workforces with them. Co-operatives are not therefore as much out of line with common practice nowadays as they were in Beatrice Webb's time. They are on the same path but further ahead. She might very well draw a different conclusion if she were writing today.

But we do agree that, even though the mental climate in industry has changed a great deal, there is still a real problem. More sophisticated skill, not less, is needed to act as a consensual manager than as an authoritarian one, and managers in a co-operative do not necessarily have it or know that they have not got it. On this point some people who start co-ops are naive. They believe that they can do without a manager at all. The Toptown printers thought that to begin with. It may, of course, be true as long as a co-op is very small and all its members are prepared to take a very full part in all its affairs but without wasting too much time in talk. But if they are not as small as that very few co-ops can be efficient without a management structure and very few of any size can get by without paying managers' salaries which can compete with what they could earn elsewhere. It also has to be accepted that the quality of management at present is often not as high as it should be.

The first task for the federation, along with the bank proposed in the next chapter, is to help those who are already doing the job. The best training would be an apprenticeship, an inexperienced manager working alongside an experienced one, either in a successful co-op or, if that is not possible, in a successful company of the ordinary sort. Short of that, a more experienced manager from outside could also be a valuable resource if he came in frequently to discuss problems or at any rate could always be telephoned for advice. Any grant to the federation would also need to be sufficient to cover the cost of such pairings.

More formal training is also needed in the practice of co-operation along with that of management. The Beechwood College in Leeds could be built up into a more fully fledged college specializing in worker co-operatives as the Co-operative College in Loughborough has specialized in consumers. The kind of course it might offer to managers and members could last, say, for a year but with only a few weeks being spent in residence at Beechwood, the rest being learning on the job, but under the guidance of a tutor from a distance. Managers would not then have to give up their ordinary jobs but could continue with them while undergoing additional training. There is much to be learnt about how to do this from the Open University and the National Extension College, both of which specialize in distance teaching. Their students do not give up their ordinary jobs if they have them but learn with the aid of correspondence courses, cassettes and videos.

Straight management training is given already in many colleges of further education, polytechnics, business schools and universities. To try and reproduce that would be folly. It would be far better to encourage managers, would-be managers and members to attend their local college if they have a suitable one, or rely on distance learning if they do not. It would also be for the federation to persuade more institutions to bring together both aspects of the training – in co-operation and in management. Business schools could do this, and colleges of further education.

The case for linking education to research is as strong for co-operation as it is in any other field of knowledge. As more research is done by the teachers and the students so will there be better material to draw on for the courses. A research institute is needed. It would collect better statistics and conduct and commission studies to find out more about the reasons for success and failure of co-operative businesses. It is sad that up to now there has been hardly a single thorough study, from the inside, of the way a successful co-operative works – the Tony Eccles study of KME is a good account of a failure. The exception is Mondragon. It has been so influential because the facts about it have been recorded. Another large subject which would repay enquiry is the different styles of co-op suitable for different kinds of people, from engineers trying to save their jobs to people trying to change the ethos of modern civilization – *Lebensreform*, to use the term adopted by the German alternative movement. Another function would be that of a clearing-house for information like the Plunkett Foundation for agricultural co-operatives.

Conclusion

Whatever is done about better training, co-ops will only expand sufficiently to form a substantial third sector if they attract many additional people of capacity and dedication. Both matter. For co-operatives at their best do represent a new way of life, at any rate of working life, and to bring that off people need to believe that work in a co-op is more than just another job.

Dedicated people will form their own networks and so increase their own solidarity. This is what happened in Spain. Father Arizmendi started with a handful of people and, long before the first co-op was set up, they devoted themselves to education and to preparation. They were the core around whom clustered more and more people impressed by the high value put on competence as well as by the solidarity which was so much in evidence. Several 'invisible colleges' (and some not so invisible) of that sort could, and we hope will, make all the difference to Britain. More and more young people, even the ones lucky enough to find employment, are dissatisfied with the old industrial order. They have rejected the relentless searching for aggrandisement which has been customary. They are ready for a more co-operative way.

6   The role of the state

Why should the state have a role at all? Co-operatives would not be co-operatives without being suspicious of it. In communist countries co-operatives are as much organs of the state as trade unions; elsewhere they are an alternative to state enterprise, challenging the mainstream socialist faith in nationalization. Why then should they plead for any help from their antagonist?

If the state was as tiny as it was when Rochdale pioneered there would be no doubt of the answer: co-operatives should look after themselves, now, as they did then. But the state has since so ramified that it has a grip upon almost every major social institution. It is not just that the state runs vast industries like the railways, coal and electricity; even under Thatcher it has a general responsibility for the manner in which the whole economy operates. If a great manufacturer like British Leyland or Rolls-Royce is threatened with collapse the state steps in to save it; if farmers need support (or say they do) the state is there to help them; if one or other region, or now the inner city, has particularly severe problems there is no one else to turn to; so it is when Britain is behind in computers or information technology. The general laws and the general taxes also bear down upon every business in the country. Co-operatives as part of society can therefore no more avoid entanglement with the state than can any other kind of business. That will be so until they succeed in the aim of reducing the role of their hoped-for benefactor.

Their stance is no different from that of private enterprise. Ordinary companies too are biased against the state. Most of their directors and managers would like to see its role cut down. But whether they like it or not, as things are, co-operatives as well as companies have to deal with the state. If they get their relationship with it wrong they can get everything wrong and their business can just as surely disappear as if the market for their goods collapsed.

Precedent of agricultural co-operatives

Governments are used to attack, even from politicians within them who manage to criticize government in general without criticizing themselves. The presence of co-ops in the chorus will not count all that much against them. But if they are asking for taxpayers' money when so many other hands are grabbing at it they will have to make out a specially good case. In doing this there is a standard rule which co-ops will ignore only at their peril. In Britain there is never any chance of doing anything new unless it is presented as not being new: it must have been done before. Fortunately there is a precedent, very much to the point, in the support the Government gives to agricultural co-operatives. In the United Kingdom over 500 of these are flourishing.

Supply co-operatives buy fertilizer, seeds, fuel, oil, machinery and hardware for their members. Marketing co-operatives sell products from the farm; their exports alone are worth nearly £1,000 million a year. The marketing boards – like the Milk Marketing Board, the Potato Marketing Board, the Hop Marketing Board and the British Wool Marketing Board – are also like producer-controlled co-operatives even though they were set up by the Government. Other co-operatives provide artificial insemination, farm secretarial services, machinery which can be hired and pest controls. Productive co-operatives process foodstuffs.

Backing all of them are support organizations of the kind we called for in the last chapter. There are, for instance, federations which do not themselves trade but represent particular types of co-op. The National Federation of Agricultural Pest Control Societies, the United Kingdom Wool Growers Federation and the Federation of Syndicate Credit Companies are examples. 'Federals' by contrast are secondary co-operatives which run new and jointly owned businesses which do not fall into any of these general categories. United Grain Producers, for example, is a joint venture set up by a number of marketing co-ops to process their grain.

All four countries of the United Kingdom have bodies representing the common interests of all kinds of agricultural co-operatives. For England this body is known as Agricultural Co-operation and Marketing Services. All four belong to the Federation of Agricultural Co-operatives for the UK as a whole.[59] There is also a well-known research organization, the Plunkett Foundation for Co-operative Studies, which collects statistics about agricultural co-operatives, holds seminars and conferences, does research and provides a consultancy service.

The depth of organization – so extensive that it is for once difficult to imagine what further cross-cutting links between co-operatives there could be – has partly been brought about by yet another body, this time one set up by the Government to promote co-operatives. The Central Council was established by the Agriculture Act of 1967. In view of what we are proposing for worker co-ops, it is worth underlining that this government body to support co-ops is quite separate from the Federation which represents them. The Central Council has a budget ten times larger than that of the Co-operative Development Agency and ten Regional Offices to give it a presence near enough to the farm-gate to make it count. Most of its money goes on capital grants.[60] But, according to John Morley who used to be Chairman of the Council, its other services have mattered more, most crucial being the free advisory and educational services for new co-ops. The Council is ready to pay for initial feasibility studies before they are established; unless they are favourable, no further money will be spent. But if they are favourable, grants can be paid out not just for equipment but for the cost of managerial and other key staff in the first three years after starting up. Such assistance can be vital.

Owing to this sort of help, agricultural co-operatives have expanded rapidly during a period when consumer co-ops have been in decline. This is, ironically, partly because of the trading done between these co-operatives and the large multiples – Sainsburys, Marks and Spencer and Tesco – which have proved such effective competitors for the retail societies.[61]

What sort of aid?

We cannot just rely on precedent. We also have to present a case for worker co-operatives on their own merits. As regards the law in general, there is one way in which co-operatives are discriminated against. Co-operatives which are registered either under the Industrial and Provident Societies Acts or as companies limited by guarantee are worse off than ordinary companies. Under the 1978 Finance Act up to £1,250 worth of shares can be issued each year free from tax to employees of a company. But these have to be irredeemable for seven years so that they cannot be cashed in and converted into tax-free income. Since shares of I and PS co-operatives are redeemable (and need to be) they are not eligible. When a co-op (other than an ICOM co-op which limits shares to one per member) issues bonus shares to its worker members they are therefore liable to pay tax at their full personal rate. This is unfair. It is all very well Treasury officials and the Registrar of Friendly Societies saying that co-operatives can issue irredeemable shares if they like and so qualify for the concession. Quite apart from anything else, this would require co-ops to change their rules. It would be more in the interest of co-operatives if the concession was extended to them provided that the bonus shares in question, though still being in principle redeemable, would not in practice be capable of being redeemed within seven years. Co-ops would then in practical terms be on all fours with companies and their members would have an extra incentive to build up their capital base.

A company has another advantage when a co-operative is being created by conversion from a traditional company. If the shares of the old company are given to a trust for the benefit of the employees of the new company, no liability to capital gains tax or capital transfer tax is incurred, although the trust is a complication which could well be done away with if there were new reforming legislation. Yet another advantage is that the initial members of a company do not have to be as many as the seven prescribed by the Industrial and Provident Societies Acts.

A 'company' is more likely to be acceptable to bank managers and the like. Companies are also cheaper to set up. So members of co-operatives are under a handicap.

In our view it would be more satisfactory if new legislation gave to existing and new co-operatives all the advantages of companies. The new Act would not refer to industrial and provident societies at all. This is a Victorian archaism. Modern co-ops are not industrial or provident societies. Partly to recognize that the reforming legislation was going to embody the best features of both Acts, the new one should be called the Co-operative Companies Act. In the course of time 'co-operative companies' would become the main term used for the legal entities established under the Act. Eventually, the great majority of co-operatives would then be registered under the same Act, and (although their constitutions would differ in detail, according to their circumstances) they would then have a legal identity in common. This would make it somewhat easier for them to recognize each other as kin and so encourage the co-operation between them for which we asked in the last chapter. It would also be easier for people outside the movement to recognize a co-operative and understand what it is, and for the Government in its dealings with the movement to know without much doubt which organization was a proper co-operative and which was not. In the interim, in giving aid and support, the Government and local authorities will have to be pragmatic about it, and decide whether a co-operative is one by its practice rather than by its legal status. Since the proposed legislation would inevitably be complicated, that interim may not be a short one. The practical steps we shall come to matter much more than legislation.

In some other countries not only have tax disabilities been removed but co-ops have been given certain tax advantages. In France, for example, bonuses paid to workers and allocated to a workers' participation fund are exempt from both corporation and personal tax as long as the fund is left intact for five years. In addition, French co-operatives may set up investment reserve funds (equal in size to the participation funds) which are also exempt from tax. Another important provision of the law in France is that workers who have been made redundant can take in advance and as a lump sum the unemployment benefit (in any case a great deal larger than it is in Britain) which they would have drawn over a period of six months and put it as capital into a co-operative or other business. Many co-operatives have been started on the strength of that money. People are by this means paid to work rather than not to work. In Britain Enterprise Allowances operate in something of the same way. But compared to France the scale is miserably small. As a nation, we still prefer to subsidize people *not* to work. Any new government in Britain would be much better advised to follow the French example.

More general discrimination

If the Government is asked to give special support to co-ops a special case has to be made out. It is, and must be, that co-ops suffer from many disadvantages which go beyond law and taxation. In everyday business practice they are discriminated against because they do not conform to the norm that people in commerce accept. 'We are a co-operative' – those words are enough to make many bank managers, accountants, solicitors, suppliers and creditors edgy. They may think of *the* co-op or of the Wedgwood Benn co-ops of the 1970s; and that could be the end of the matter. Or they may take it for granted that any firm which has participatory management is bound to fail. To succeed, they may think, there must be a boss whose power over *his* concern cannot be challenged. Clearly, it may make or break the co-op if it is refused an outside loan which would otherwise have been granted just because it has no conventional boss, or if it fails to get credit which would have been given to someone else, or, indeed, to get a contract because, in a capitalist world, its very name makes it suspect.

There is no doubt of the relative disadvantage and of the need for the different attitude of which David Owen wrote:

> The central issue that must be faced is that if industrial co-operatives are to expand, and if their ethos is to influence the general industrial climate, then they will have to benefit from positive discrimination.

The faint hearts will argue that all sectors of the economy should be treated the same, but all governments have discriminated in the past between the private or public sectors and when socialist governments are quite prepared to legislate for the nationalisation of whole industries, and to pay a high price in compensation, it is amazing that there has been, in relative terms, so little legislative support for industrial co-operatives.[62]

The case for such positive discrimination does not have to be made out for farmers, because, of course, farmers have votes concentrated in rural constituencies, which makes them a powerful political force even in Britain which has proportionately fewer of them than any other country in the world. Workers also have votes but there are not so many of them in co-operatives, at least for the moment. But their case is strong. We have referred before to some of the main elements in it and now bring them together.

1 The mix we have had between state and private enterprise has not been exactly a brilliant success. One reason is that both have been divided and embittered by their two 'sides'. Co-operatives could add to the economy a form of enterprise relatively free from that endemic conflict which has become so much more crippling now that it gives so much extra impetus to inflation. If co-operatives had more weight in the economy generally and lived up to their name they could be an example for the whole of industry.

2 For reasons going to the heart of modern society (even in countries like West Germany whose industrial success has been outstanding) there has been a shift in values. More people, particularly younger ones, want less hierarchy at work than in the past. The state should provide a favourable environment for them just as it did for capitalism by its creation of the limited liability company.

3 Some of the people most susceptible to this shift in values would not enter business at all, and so create jobs for themselves and for others, unless into some form of co-operative. To aid them would be to reduce unemployment. Co-operatives are generally labour-intensive.

4 A firm owned by its workers has a special attraction for local authorities. If it is owned and controlled, as it must be, by local people, it is not liable to be closed down by some distant head office. It is more likely to respect its local responsibilities and more likely, as a consequence, to attract local cash.

5 Co-ops, like many infant firms, have been trapped in a vicious circle. Without a track record, they cannot get money; without money they cannot get a track record. Some special assistance may be the only way to break out of the circle.

What sort of intervention?

If the arguments are accepted, what should the Government do? To answer we begin with the functions before considering *who* should perform them. There are two principal ones – consultancy and financial – apart from the training considered in the last chapter.

Of the two, consultancy, if given a wide meaning, is far and away the most important. Whether new starts, conversions or rescues, the need of all new co-ops is for the best possible commercial advice. Assessment of the prospects for the business is always necessary and this depends crucially upon the state of the market. So the extent of the competition, from overseas firms as well as British, has to be measured, which can only be done by getting access to the sort of information possessed by the Caja or by one of the Japanese banks which we shall mention in a moment.

Getting the right manager matters more than anything else. One of the great assets of co-ops is that they attract enthusiasts. But fine as that is, enthusiasts are finer still if they have had business experience. When they have had none, or not enough, they have to look for someone from outside who has been a manager before. This is where a consultancy service could be so useful. It could maintain a register of people with suitable skills. From that could sometimes come the managerial talent without which the whole venture might collapse. A consultant could also advise on the management structure to give the manager the authority that is necessary and allow every member to play his or her part in decision-making. On all such matters advice and encouragement will be needed on a continuing basis. The worst troubles may only emerge when the first flush of enthusiasm is over.

Where are all the consultants to come from? Obviously it will not be simple to find them, and quite impossible in a short period. They will be accountants, engineers, lawyers and the like who take a course on co-operatives. Few of them will know much about co-operative companies to begin with. In the longer run more and more younger people or people converting in mid-life should graduate from the courses for co-operative consultants which it is hoped that one or more of the business schools will provide.

The new bank

Finance also matters, of course. A financial institution whose staff are knowledgeable about co-operatives will be a necessity. Let us call it a bank.

What would the bank do? It would not be like the Caja in one respect, for it would certainly not handle the current accounts of co-operatives. The Co-operative Bank and the ordinary high street banks already do this. They have local branches and there would be no point in the new bank competing with them for such ordinary services.

It would also not be like the Caja in supplying all the outside capital. The new bank would not find all that was needed apart from that provided by the members themselves. The task would be to work out the most favourable financial package, with contributions on the best terms that could be negotiated from merchant banks, pension funds, ordinary banks and other specialized financial institutions. The new bank could regard itself as a banker of last resort which would often need to put in some of its own money in order to bring in and encourage others, in this like the National Consumer Co-operative Bank which – despite its name – was set up by the US Government partly to support worker co-ops.[63]

The next question, in three parts, is about who should do it. Should the federation be responsible for both these functions? If not, should the responsibility for consultancy be separated from finance? Either way, whose should be the responsibility?

On the first matter European experience is not decisive. In France, SCOP has money from the Government but it is not enough to add anything substantial to the investment fund it has accumulated from its own members. The Italian federations have also received government money. Mondragon is no guide either way because before the bank there was no federation, nothing to give money to even had there been a government willing to give it. When the bank started up it did so in order to perform the two functions together.

But the crucial point is that the British Government does not usually make grants to bodies over which it has no control. The federation would be a representative body and governed by the members whom it was representing. To give it investment funds and ask the elected council which of their members should get the money would inevitably be embarrassing. However much they tried to keep internal politics out of financial decisions they would sometimes (often? always?) fail. The money could be divided up between factions. Or if politics could be kept out of it there would still be no reason why a council which was elected to represent and campaign would have at its disposal the right skills to distribute money wisely, or, indeed, to decide who was to get the benefit of any consultancy services available.

Furthermore, to promote the interests of its members the federation should be free to attack the Government whenever that was thought necessary and should certainly not feel restrained because it was receiving money from it. On its side the Government should not be deterred from finding funds for new co-ops because it was out of sympathy with the stand taken by the federation.

If the federation is ruled out, is there another body which should have both functions? The orthodox British view is that the two functions should be kept apart. It is that consultants give advice to managers and it is then up to the managers whether to accept or reject it. It is thought that if consultants had the power of the purse as well, that could give them too much influence;

they could be too much feared and so too little trusted with confidences. The ordinary conclusion is that advice should be the province of consultants and decisions about money that of the people who make the financial assessments. Despite this being the standard practice, we believe that for our purpose consultancy and finance should not be separate but together, as at Mondragon and at the Central Council or in a different way at the Highlands and Islands Development Board.

Our fear is the opposite of the orthodox view. Unless they belong to the same organization as the bank, or are at least commissioned by it, the consultants, far from having too much influence with the co-operatives they serve, will not have enough. The success of Mondragon is due in some part to the discipline exercised by the bank over the individual co-operatives. We do not expect anything quite as tight as that in Britain. But we do expect that co-operatives which get government finance should be under a good deal of discipline all the same. They should not be able to say to the consultants, no, we will keep the management structure we have got even if you think it will make us fail; or no, we do not intend to appoint a sales manager, the sales will look after themselves; or no, we do not intend to seek out new markets, we are quite satisfied with what we have got. They should not be able to say all these things and still get the money. Support would be conditional upon their acting on the consultant's advice, of course after discussing it. The experience is that co-operatives are liable to have weak management. To strengthen it the consultants will need all the muscle that influence over money would give them.

Such a bank, with consultants on its staff, sharing the responsibility for assessing financial needs, would not be like other British banks. One of their stock defects – unlike Japanese and German banks which have made a practice of investing in industry – is that they are often unable to say anything except yes, we will give you a loan or an overdraft, or no, we will not. They do not give regular advice to their customers about how to improve their businesses. They do not employ the people who would be able to give such advice and if they did and tried to they would often be told to mind their own business, not their customer's.

Japanese practice is relevant in another way as well. Most Japanese companies are formed into 'co-operatives', not our sort but co-operatives of companies. The first kind of group or co-operative is the descendant of pre-war family holding companies. Mitsubishi is perhaps the best-known example, with Mitsubishi companies in car manufacturing and a host of other industries often without the Mitsubishi name – such as Kirin beer, Asahi Glass and NYK in the merchant marine. The second kind consists of a major manufacturer and its related subsidiaries, a large company like Nissan, Hitachi, Sony or Matsushita Electric also having large numbers of non-competing firms in their groups which, while having their own independent management, co-operate between each other in almost every possible way. The third group is the one most immediately to the point for us, the group led by a bank. The bank lends money to the companies in its group, owns shares in them and, again, does all it can to promote co-operation between them, persuading them to buy and sell to each other, to set up common selling arrangements especially in export markets, to help each other with research, to get orders and, above all, to exchange information.[64] Banks are not only suppliers of finance; they do what they can to make their customers flourish. They are the middlemen of inter-company co-operation.

One example is the Shoko Chukin Bank (Central Bank for Commerce and Industry). The big businesses of Japan are now world-famous. The small ones are not. But there are nearly six million of them, and amongst small businesses in manufacturing 50 per cent are members of co-operatives. This bank has 26,000 member co-operatives as customers, and 150,000 companies are members of one or other of them. The bank will not lend more than £4 million (one-fifth of the sum we are proposing should to begin with be spent on co-operatives for the whole of Britain) to any one of the 26,000 member co-operatives to finance the services they offer their members. The bank has a free consultancy service and a massive computerized information service. If a member firm wants to know how many cotton socks were imported into Britain last year, and from where, it will be able to obtain the information within a few minutes on its video screen. How long would it take a British bank to answer the same question for its own country?

The Japanese example points to the same conclusion as the Caja. They both work not just directly through their own staff but by encouraging co-operation for their mutual benefit between their customers. Ularco could be a good model and Shoko Chukin another – that is for the encouragement of groupings between vertically linked co-operatives and non-competitive ones in a particular industry. One notable example in Britain is the 'Cambridge Co-operative', as it is called, a loose association of more than eighty companies in computer and other high-technology industries operating around the University at Cambridge.

The candidates

On the third question about whose the responsibility should be, something quite new would only be worth contemplating if nothing existed at present which could do the job and, since there are a number of strong candidates already in the field, that would be difficult to argue. The first is the Co-operative Bank. This we rule out on the grounds that if it had government funds to dispense it would have a privileged position in relation to other commercial banks with which it competes. Such a privilege would be difficult to defend. It also has little in the way of a consultancy service at present. ICOF (Industrial Common Ownership Finance) has a claim too. It has been doing just the job we are specifying, although on a very small scale and with a very small staff. It is in fact so small that it would hardly provide a suitable base from which the much larger organization we have in mind could be built.

That leaves three main contenders, the Industrial and Commercial Finance Corporation, the British Technology Group and the Co-operative Development Agency. ICFC has the right kind of experience, and much of it. It is a kind of bank (at least on the Japanese and German model) which provides long-term risk capital for small and medium-sized businesses; it had £420 million invested in 3,500 companies in Britain in the year ending March 1981. In that same year it invested £28 million in 400 start-ups, of which 260 were brand new ones. It has eighteen area offices in major towns with staff drawn from science and engineering as well as law and accountancy and a large consultancy division with people experienced in engineering, accounting, marketing, production and property. It is strong in new technology, having a wholly owned subsidiary in Technical Development Capital Ltd which specializes in very high financial risks, and it is also a leader in the management buy-outs which we refer to later. But ICFC has no experience of co-operatives and was not set up by the Government, being part of the Finance for Industry group which is 85 per cent owned by the English and Scottish clearing banks and 15 per cent by the Bank of England.

Its weakness from our point of view is that lack of experience of co-operatives which it might not wish to remedy. No government could instruct it to do so but might be able to persuade it. If successful, this would almost certainly mean setting up a co-operative division which would be able to make use of the main consultancy service and the staff of the area offices as well as the general information store available to the whole organization.

The British Technology Group *is* a government body, which has brought together the National Enterprise Board and the National Research and Development Corporation. The Group will continue to invest government money in new kinds of business, especially in growth sectors where Britain has been lagging. It will also continue, on an increasing scale, the work that the National Research and Development Corporation has done since the war in building commercial assets out of research done in universities and public authorities. The new Chairman said in the 1981 Report that 'an organisation with a strong commercial bias and a clear responsibility to pull through inventions from the Universities to the shop floor is needed if Britain is not to continue to underexploit its greatest national asset – the inventive genius of its people'. The Group has regional offices in England and an office in Scotland, although not so many as ICFC. Since it is a government body already it would without any great adaptation be able to take on the additional responsibility of looking after co-operatives, although it would also presumably have to set up a special division for the purpose just as ICFC would. It does not possess ready-made the sort of consultancy service that ICFC has nor the same experience in starting and supporting small businesses. Of the two, ICFC seems to be the stronger candidate.

The Co-operative Development Agency is the other main contender and the only one of the three which would jump at the chance of being chosen. It has an asset which neither of the other two possesses – a knowledge of co-operatives and a commitment to their expansion. Its liability is that it does not have the commercial experience of financing new co-operatives nor of providing consultancy support for them except on a small scale. Whether it can under its new leadership overcome this handicap, or show good prospects of doing so, has yet to be demonstrated. If it does, it will have a good claim to be *the* body, and as such could try and negotiate an agreement with ICFC for access to its consultancy service. It would need to change its name, say to the Bank for Co-operative Development.

If the responsibility did not go wholly one way or another the CDA could advise and finance smaller co-operatives, say those with less than twenty-five members, and ICFC the larger ones. But when worker co-ops taken together are still so small, and few new ones start with more than twenty-five members, it would be a pity to divide functions in this way. At the national level it would be better to have one body than two.

In arranging the conversion of businesses into co-ops the bank could in the course of time become the acknowledged specialist. Many, if not most, new businesses go through the same cycle which is related to the cycle of family life. They are started by an individual proprietor and, if they survive, they expand up to a point without his having to give away control. He retains the sole or main shareholding even if he takes on a manager or other people to help him. The business reaches a critical period when it is faced with the problems of the succession. Will it remain a family business or not? Any family business is very like a dictatorship which is rocked, sometimes almost to the point of dissolution, when the dictator dies or becomes incapable. Any organization heavily dependent upon a single person who has not arranged for an orderly succession is liable to the same disability.

All is well if the proprietor not only has children but at least one who is able and willing to be trained and to take over when the father dies or retires. It may not matter all that much if the transition is very sudden as long as there is an heir. All may also be well if the proprietor is ready to take in a younger partner, as it will if he himself sells out or converts the company into a public one. He can then take money out of it which he can pass on to his children even if they do not want money's-worth in the shape of the business. But if he does not want the cash and has no suitable heir, what then? He may well be attached to his employees and be happy to transfer the business to them if only he can be reasonably assured that there can be some continuity of management. We have had the examples already of Scott Bader and John Lewis where there were sons and they followed the father not into a capitalist but into a co-operative kind of business. Many other firms, usually smaller, have been left without suitable family heirs and the firms have been sold to or given to the employees. There could be many more like that in the future, and the bank, by specializing in this kind of conversion and making the fact known, could multiply the number. A worthwhile step would be to get in touch with all businesses above a certain size which had been in existence for, say, twenty years and according to the records held by the Companies' Registrar had a single proprietor – if that would not make the bank appear too much like an undertaker who is on the scene to offer his future services well before the time when he would (however sadly) be welcome.

The other speciality for the bank could be the rescues to which we have already devoted a great deal of attention. As long as the number of bankruptcies remains anywhere near its present height there will be plenty of scope. Once it became known that the bank was prepared to consider requests from employees it could be besieged. But a first sieving should show up the companies which could stand up again in new clothes.

A general point to make about rescues is that they often come too late; where the patient is dead or nearly dead all the money in the world could not revive him. If only the effort could come earlier it would have more chance of success. Bearing this in mind, could the bank contrive to get in earlier than happens at the moment when there is going to be a closure? Liquidation is the last resort when a company fails. Can there be a penultimate resort? Not too close to the ultimate?

We are not for a moment denying the vulnerability of any concern which is failing, at whatever point it may be on the downward slope. The reasons for its being there at all have to be sought for and if they are 'good' ones (that is, bad for the concern) it is a matter for a funeral rather than a co-operative. We are not denying that. We are asserting merely that, other things being equal, to get in earlier is better than to get in later. The business will not have lost so many of its customers, managers, or most effective workers; nor will it have lost so much of its credit, reputation and morale.

If action can be taken early enough a policy directed to that end makes more sense than one designed to foster the promotion of new co-operatives from scratch. Many new firms, co-operatives or any other, are, sadly, on the way to collapse; and too often too soon. An existing concern, on the other hand, even if it is moving towards failure, has certain assets which the entirely new concern is without, above all a body of employees who can exert themselves, if they have the will and the leadership, to save themselves. A new firm has at the beginning only a potential body of that sort, not a ready-made one, and therefore does not have the advantage of having a group of people behind it fighting in their own defence. They can also raise allies in their community or nationally, and, often mattering more than that, they may also have allies inside a parent group which has decided to close one of its plants.

If the bank's existence and its interest was known, and if it was also known that information could be given to it in confidence, with no more risk of being passed on to anyone else than similar information passed to any other banker, some information would come its way in any event. At present there is under Section 99 of the Employment Protection Act a duty on employers to notify the Secretary of State of impending redundancies within 90 days if 100 or more workers are employed and within 60 days if 10 or more are employed. We suggest that in addition to this some new duties should be placed on companies, and public sector bodies for that matter, to give similar or even longer notice of an expected closure which is going to make a sizeable number of people redundant.

It will be different for an entire company which is going into liquidation than for a national or multi-national company with plants or offices in several locations which is going to close one of them. The first kind may be hit by a sudden storm and have to cease business with very little warning if only in the interest of its creditors. If the company itself only has a month's warning of its own demise it cannot give more than that. Not so with the second kind. It would still exist as an entity subject to British law after the proposed closure unless, as a multi-national, it withdrew completely from the UK. It could be required not to close a plant unless the period of notice had been given and discussions held with the bank.

There are, of course, objections to requiring anything of the sort, particularly because the new bank would not be able to do anything effective to keep the business going and to convert it into a co-operative without the support of the company concerned. Unless within the management of that company there was some willingness to keep the plant open, nothing to good effect would happen anyway. Without some goodwill on the part of the management and the workforce the vital feasibility study that would always be needed could not be made. The management, even though it had failed or was about to, would know the facts of the business in a way no outsider could. A change in product would often be necessary at least when a plant in a multi-location company was involved and when the closure was to be made in order to concentrate production in fewer plants than before. The company might not be willing to allow the product which it had developed to be made by a new and potentially competitive concern.

Whether or not there was any compulsion about the period of notice, no company would be willing to deal with the bank unless to do so served its own company interests. Apart from the goodwill that a large company at any rate would attract if it showed itself keen to try and save the jobs of its employees, the incentive would have to be cash. The bank would therefore have to be ready to put up a proposition for a workers' buy-out and to place a price on the assets of the company higher than would be obtained if the company went into liquidation. Its value as a going concern would normally be higher than that. But the fact that the bank could if it wished bide its time and wait for the liquidation should mean that the price would not be all that much higher.

We have been talking about companies before they reach the point of liquidation. When they have got that far, we think the employees should have special rights. The law on insolvency has recently been reviewed by the Cork Committee:

> It became clear at an early stage of our deliberations that the immense social and economic changes which have taken place since the mid-Nineteenth Century, when our present insolvency laws and procedures were formulated, have rendered them at best obsolescent and at worse positively harmful. Without radical reform they are no longer capable of meeting the requirements of a modern society and fresh legislation of a comprehensive nature is urgently required.[65]

One of the most important changes of recent times is the increase in the extent to which capital is raised by means of secured loans from banks and other lenders. As well as giving the bank a charge on the assets, small businessmen, and sometimes the members of a co-operative, are told that they must give personal guarantees as well. This means that if things go wrong they can lose their houses and everything else they own, forfeiting the protection of limited liability. Where banks have a floating charge, as they usually do, this ensures that they have priority over most other debtors. The rights of ordinary creditors and of workers (apart from wages owed to them and their redundancy money) are pushed to one side.

Many reforms are needed. One is that workers should always be invited by the liquidator to put in a bid for the assets of the company when and if they are sold, and if the workers are offering a price comparable to that of other buyers they should be given preference. One of the duties of the new bank would be to help workers, through their unions or on their own, to prepare the plans on which such bids would be based. Jobs would then more often be saved instead of assets being stripped and machinery and other equipment sold, quite often to be sent overseas at knock-down prices.

Workforce buy-outs

When a closure is on the way a workforce buy-out should be considered as one of the possible ways of averting it. This is a variation on the management buy-out which has become increasingly common. The growth in the number of them handled by ICFC alone has grown as follows:

	Number of buy-outs	ICFC sums invested
1977–8	10	not known
1978–9	20	£3.2 m
1979–80	49	£11.6 m
1980–1	69	£15.5 m

A buy-out may come about for a number of different reasons. A parent company – multi-national or British – may decide to close down or sell a UK division: the division may no longer fit into the company's strategic plans, or may not be profitable enough; a newly acquired company may contain unwanted elements, or the parent company may just need to raise cash. Or the shareholders of a private company – unlike the single proprietor being considered earlier – may wish to sell out completely. In such cases the managers, not at all wanting to be shuffled off as though they did not count, may be prepared to put in a bid themselves. If they succeed they will not only manage the business, but own it. The vendors may be quite happy as long as they can get as good a price as they could from anyone else, and perhaps happier if they avoid the odium of selling out over the heads of the management and keep suppliers and customers friendly. Employees obviously want their jobs to be saved and customers have a like interest because they usually do not want their supplies to be cut off. Every bankruptcy is not only bad for the firm closed down. It is also bad for other companies who have, perhaps very quickly, to find other suppliers of highly specialized materials or semi-finished products.

The knock-on effect of the closure of any firm can also be even more severe for that firm's suppliers. The loss of part of their market can put them too into a spin from which they cannot recover. A whole local economy may then be plunged into an accelerating decline as first one firm closes, then its suppliers and then the suppliers of those suppliers. As the number of local redundancies mounts there is less money to spend in local shops and local services and so other firms in that sector also collapse, pushing demand down still further. But if only the firm can be kept in existence these knock-on effects can be avoided. The new bank would more than justify itself if by its intervention it saved even a few local economies from this kind of collapse.

Professor Mitchell has summed up the case for mounting rescues before it is too late.

> One advantage of setting up a business based on an old one, or rescuing the best bits from a disaster, is that one is starting a business part way up the learning curve. The learning curve includes the length of time needed to run a new business in and the associated costs of setting the venture on its path. New contracts have to be made, managers and work force learn the job. Buyouts can avoid some of the costs, and cut down running-in times. Some start-up costs may also be avoided such as the need for new premises; promotion costs for entry into new markets, or in relationships with suppliers. Buyouts can also preserve some of the value of what has gone before.[66]

But can the managers raise the cash? Ordinarily they cannot, out of their own resources or by borrowing on mortgages and the like. Typically, they can find 10 per cent or 20 per cent of the funds. The rest has to come from a body like ICFC and could come from the Bank for Co-operative Development as well, if it existed. Such a body could lend the rest of the money, mostly by way of loan on the security of the assets of the company, some in the form of a 'royalty' or the like on the lines of the Barclays Bank Business Start Loan mentioned in Chapter 3.

So far there have been very few workers' buy-outs with all the employees, rather than just the managers, contributing cash. As an article in the *Financial Times* put it: 'In some cases they thought of setting up a co-operative, but decided that it would be easier both to manage the business and to find financial backers if they stuck to the more widely accepted limited company form of association, instead of venturing out into the more controversial and less understood area of co-ops.'[67] If the people concerned *had* known that they could have set up a limited company form of co-operative they might have come to a different conclusion.

A near-miss of this sort was Panache Upholstery in Leeds. The fifty-five former employees of the predecessor company lent £61,000 interest-free – all their redundancy pay – to Panache. The former accountant and sales director became the managing director of the new company and ICFC lent him and them the bulk of the money to buy the assets and put them into a new company which stopped just short of being a co-operative. Peterlee Wallpaper had a similar story. Its twenty employees raised £45,000 in redundancy pay and other savings in the form of an equity stake so that they could buy the business when closure was inevitable. They elected three specialist managers to be directors and at the suggestion of ICFC, who lent the rest of the money needed for the purchase, hired an outsider as non-executive chairman. New employees are invited but not compelled to invest in the company.

In such cases the new bank, sometimes working alongside ICFC, could at least try to make sure that the employees knew about co-operative companies. A workforce buy-out leading to a co-operative would then be one of the options for people to consider. Managers would not necessarily be against it. They would not, of course, have as many votes at the annual general meeting as in a company they owned and might be voted off the board of directors. But as long as they were doing a reasonable job this would be unlikely to happen. The positive advantages for the managers should be that if all 'employees' were also members, with the same voting rights, there should be a better chance of avoiding the gulf between managers and workers which has been such a curse for so long. The time saved in dealing with industrial relations could be a major advantage.

Such rescues do not have to be confined to the private sphere. The largest buy-out of recent years was in the public sector. Inside every large company is a small company trying to get out. This also applies to the great domain of the Department of Industry. The National Freight Corporation, far and away the largest road haulier in the country, was a nationalized industry which the Thatcher Government was determined to privatize.

Knowing this, and fearing that the Government might sell them up piecemeal with the loss of many jobs, the managers, led by their chief executive, Mr Peter Thompson, decided to put together a bid of their own. The senior managers came forward with most of the money, the other managers with less, and more than half of the 24,000 other employees advanced an average of £719 each. Between them the managers and employees control much more than half the equity of £7.5 million. Most of the rest of the £53.5 million which had to be paid to the Government came not from ICFC but from a group of City institutions headed by Barclays Merchant Bank.

The NFC is not a co-operative. Not all employees are shareholders and votes vary with the size of the shareholdings. But it has some of the same characteristics. Most of the workers *are* shareholders and the managers have to remember it. This fact helps to encourage the kind of participative management which Mr Thompson favours. 'An authoritarian management could not', he says, 'contemplate being answerable to thousands of shareholders who were also their subordinates at work.'[68] It would not have been beyond the bounds of belief for the NFC to have been born as a full co-operative.

This example also suggests what might happen in other nationalized industries, especially where some parts could be divided off from the whole without reducing efficiency. Worker co-operatives could, for instance, tender for the catering services on trains and stations and for taking over branch lines which might otherwise be closed. Railway enthusiasts have set up what are in effect co-operatives of an unusual kind to take over some such branch lines. Why not worker co-operatives? In Italy the permanent way is not maintained by the staff employed direct by the railways but by a large worker co-operative as well as other outside contractors. There is surely scope for emulation in Britain. The same thing could happen with local electricity distribution[69] or British Rail hotels or some of the services of the National Bus Company or with airports. Certain services of local authorities could be treated in the same way. Tenant management co-operatives in some places already perform the functions which used to belong to housing departments. Nurseries and nursery schools have been created as co-operatives. No local authority has yet gone as far as some Italian ones which have given contracts to social work co-operatives.[70] Perhaps that day too will come.

Outside the public services there could be much parallel development in the private sector which, without going as far as co-ops, will be directed to the same end of enlarging participation. This can be buttressed by profit-sharing and by partial employee ownership of shares. An ordinary company could not only take all the steps it could under the Finance Act of 1978 to enable workers to buy shares in it and to gain all the attendant tax advantages but could also go further and set up its own 'wages fund'.[71] Such a fund would be made up of a proportion of profits set aside each year and used to purchase shares on the market which would be held in trust for the workers until such time as they owned a controlling stake in their company. This could lead eventually to their owning all the shares. The present Swedish Government is committed to a variation of this known as the Meidner plan. The extension of share ownership could help, in however small a way, to reduce the disharmony in industry, especially if full co-operatives were growing all the time in number, scope and influence so that there was overall a strong sense of movement towards a new order in industry. It should always be the case that co-operatives offer a model of participation to all the rest, so much so that more and more companies convert of their own volition. The theory is already attractive. Now needed more than anything else is a series of successes, including some substantial ones. Actions will, as always, speak louder than words.

Conclusion

We have been recommending a new regime for supporting the co-operative companies of the future, well knowing that whether it will be considered a worthwhile 'investment' by the Government will depend in good part upon how large that investment is. It is not possible to put any very precise figures upon it at present, partly because so much will depend upon the numbers of experienced staff who will be willing to join the new bank including the consultancy service. The Empresarial Division of the Caja doing consultancy in the broadest sense of the term (including forecasting, business planning, auditing) for all the Mondragon co-operatives has a staff of 115. Our new Bank for Co-operative Development will not, at the national level, be able to reach that size right away. But if the bank was able to start off with a staff of 70 consultants and bankers, with salaries, national insurance and support costs for each being on average £30,000, the cost of the consultancy service would be about £2 million a year at present prices. How much for capital? In 1980–1 grants of £2.4 million were made to farm co-ops under the agricultural and horticultural co-operative scheme. Farming is only a small part of the economy, whereas the new bank will be open to applications from anyone. A bottom limit for the first year covering all industries and services would be at least £20 million apart from any grant direct to the federation. This is less than the subsidy paid each year to just one state-owned company, British Leyland, but considerably larger than the £200,000 p.a. which is the government grant at present being received by the CDA.

Is it too much to hope that the state should spend such a sum on a very different sort of enterprise from British Leyland? All we can say is that, from our particular point of view, it would be very much the right action to take. It would be pump-priming money. Some of it would be wasted, inevitably. But if people of experience, enthusiasm and imagination could be brought together into a team spanning the country, not just concentrated in London, it could produce a large advance in a comparatively short period. Heavy unemployment for a long time ahead is likely. That unemployment is due in part to the rigidities which have grown ever greater in the old economic order. It is a time both for taking new initiatives and for re-taking old initiatives in a new form.

7 The new mechanized peasantry

We start in this final chapter by broadening out from paid work to include unpaid work as well. This we do because our first thesis is that, in the great trade-off of modern society, people have by and large traded away the satisfaction they get from their paid work in order to gain more satisfaction in their unpaid. Ordinary jobs have become less interesting but better paid and the extra money has been used to make domestic jobs more interesting. The stereotype is not just the telly-watcher slumped in his chair but the worker in a factory who downs tools the moment the clock strikes four so that he can hurry home to take out his own tools from their chest or shed to make, with loving care, a new piece of furniture for his kitchen, to transplant his tomato seedlings from his greenhouse or to repair the car which shuttles him back and forth between one workplace and another. There is no need to ask which work people are most attached to – being employed by someone else or self-employed, with only wife or husband or children to chivvy or be chivvied by. Read the face; look in the mirror – unless, that is, you belong to the lucky (or unlucky?) minority whose paid work demands as much skill as any DIY and is therefore as absorbing.

This matters so much for co-operatives because if the same great trade-off persists as tenaciously as it has done so far, then prospects for co-operatives are that much bleaker. Their purpose is to make work more meaningful, more worthwhile, more fulfilling. The command structure, on which we have been concentrating so far, is one of the main obstacles in the way. Workers who are always told what to do by a boss – treated in other ways as though they are more or less intelligent but always biddable machines or as second-rate human beings – are bound to resent it in some degree or another. Despite the political democracy which has been won, and the liberties that go with it, we still live to a very large extent in an 'on-behalf' society where decisions are taken on behalf of us instead of *by* us.

So there is much to be said for co-operatives if they can make the command structure itself more biddable; and some of it we have tried to say. Yet we have to accept that the introduction of a variant of democracy into working life would not of itself do all that much – though it should do something – to add to the satisfaction to be gained from work. The analogy with political government is uncomfortably close. Political democracy is the least bad system of government yet devised. It places limits on the extent to which rulers can become tyrants. But democracy does not make governments loved, or even liked, or worth striving for yourself unless you happen to be a political animal, in which case you do not engage in politics because you choose to but because you have to. Apathy is the word applied by such animals to their brethren who show a disinclination to sit in election cars roaring into the night air. Apathy is the word to describe people who listen rather than speak.

The analogy is close because there is no reason to expect people to believe that government is the noblest art of man, a grand march through an infinity of compromises, just because autocracy is replaced by democracy in industry. This they will only do if the activity which is being governed is such as to quicken the imagination and stir the feelings. The point can be made less extravagantly by enunciating the Young and Rigge law – the more people care about work, the keener they will be to participate in its management.

The reason for putting it this way is that, unless there is willingness on the part of workers to engage themselves as active citizens in the democracy of work, no co-operative will live up to its promise. The workers, though not called that but members, could be almost as ready to leave their common affairs to be controlled by 'the management', that is by someone else, not themselves, as they are in an ordinary concern in the first and second sectors. They could still be more onlookers than partici-pators – the victims of the 'iron law of organizations', which is that managers concentrate power by inducing indifference.

Michels said about trade unions what he could have said with equal justification about almost any other large organization, that the majority of members are as indifferent to the organization as the majority of electors are to Parliament.[72]

What we have lost

Could the trend be bucked? To assess the chances of paid work capturing some of the joys of the unpaid variety we need to consider how deep-seated is the present trend. It is no use crying out for a radical change if the work–leisure compromise is the best that man can currently achieve.

The trend *is* deep-seated, no doubt about that. The riches which have paid for the tools used at home and the dullness which so many jobs inspire are both products of the modern division of labour. The division of labour is the source of wealth of nations as well as of greater alienation from the work that creates it. To take the measure of the change you only have to look back a century or two.

Before the invention of the machines which in Marx's words could 'spin without fingers' the man who worked the land had an even bigger range of jobs than a modern agricultural worker because he had to do so many of them by hand, like cutting the corn, winnowing it or preparing the straw for storage; and his wife was often not just a housewife but a baker, a poultry-woman, a cider-maker, a cheese and butter-maker, a beekeeper, a milkmaid. But in industry the generalist was gradually ousted by the specialist. Adam Smith is famous for his demonstration of the superior efficiency of the division of labour even in the eighteenth century, with his example, chosen for its unlikeliness, being the manufacture of about the tiniest product of all, the pin. A thousand ideologues danced on the point of that pin, in the most famous factory there has ever been, where fragmentation of the enormous process of making a pin was subdivided into eighteen different operations 'which in some manufactories are all performed by distinct hands, though in others the same man will sometimes perform two or three of them'.

Adam Smith, if he did not actually imagine himself into the

mind of a man who gives the same twist to his wrist 15,000 times a day, at least recognized the costs as well as the benefits of the division of labour.

> The man whose whole life is spent in performing a few simple operations, of which the effects too are perhaps always the same, or very nearly the same, has no occasion to exert his understanding or to exercise his invention in finding out expedients for removing difficulties which never occur. He naturally loses, therefore, the habit of such exertion, and generally becomes as stupid and ignorant as it is possible for a human creature to become.[73]

He was speaking of manual workers. Peter Kropotkin at the end of the last century widened the attack to cover much of what goes on in society as a whole.

> And the division and subdivision – the permanent subdivision – of functions has been pushed so far as to divide humanity into castes which are almost as firmly established as those in old India. We have, first, the broad division into producers and consumers: little-consuming producers on the one hand, little-producing consumers on the other hand. Then, amidst the former, a series of further subdivisions: the manual worker and the intellectual worker, sharply separated from one another to the detriment of both; the agricultural labourers and the workers in the manufacture; and, amidst the mass of the latter, numberless subdivisions again – so minute, indeed, that the modern ideal of a workman seems to be a man or a woman, or even a girl or a boy, without the knowledge of any handicraft, without any conception whatever of the industry he or she is employed in, who is only capable of making all day long and for a whole life the same infinitesimal part of something; who from the age of 13 to that of 60 pushes the coal cart at a given spot of the mine or makes the spring of a penknife, or 'the eighteenth part of a pin'.[74]

The striking thing about such comments is that they have dated so little. There are also still millions of jobs with far too much of the repetitious about them to hold interest for long, being now perhaps even more common in offices than they are in factories or in transport. For offices are under the sway of specialization. The same people do not ordinarily clean them, paint them, man the switchboard, photocopier and computers, do the typing, the shorthand, the longhand, the accounting, the despatching, the committeeing, receiving, repairing, ordering.

The harvest

The miracles of organization and reorganization in this century have not until recently produced small units but their opposite in the towering office blocks and strung-out factories of a uniform urbanized society which stretches from Seoul to Sunderland and Berlin to Bristol and almost all points in between. The consequences have been dire, for work as it is ordinarily understood. The system, supported of course by its command structure, removes from most people the choice of what they shall make, the choice of how they shall make it and sometimes the skill that was once needed to make it. All this is possible in and out of factories because (as Marx said) people sell their labour-power: it is all they have to sell. That is certainly one way of putting it. We prefer to talk about time, because to do so brings out the extent to which people are slaves, not masters. People sell their time: it is the most precious possession they have to sell. In exchange for the money they earn they give other people, or they give the system, the right to control what they do with their time. By and large they seem to be more productive if they repeat what they do again and again until they are action- or sometimes word-perfect. Their time is chopped up into little pieces, with the same job being done again and again throughout the hour, the day, the week, the year, the life. People are surrendering their scarcest possession in order to have it fragmented by a boss or a system and so to have themselves chopped into little pieces.

But they are surrendering it willingly, for the sake of the money which their greater 'efficiency' entitles them to. The money buys them the freedom to be their own masters and mistresses doing their own work in a state of self-employment at home, or if not self-employed then employment within the informal co-operative of the family. The division of labour associated with mechanization in the sphere of production has brought about its opposite in the sphere of consumption.

In an earlier phase of industrialization the large scale in production was matched by the large scale in consumption. Almost everything was collective. The water used to come from a collective well or stand-pipe in the street. The washing was done in communal wash-places; people used public slipper-baths; travelled on buses and trains; went to music-halls, theatres and then cinemas. But in the phase we are now in, a society of still-large factories and offices has become a society of miniature life on the scale of the household. Water, gas and electricity have piped essentials into the home. The mechanical mower has replaced the manual in the garden. The fractional horse-power motor has powered home laundries where there used to be commercial ones, home ice-makers where there used to be ice-factories, freezers where there used to be cold stores. The average housewife has been given 'about the same amount of mechanical assistance (about two horsepower) as was deployed by the average industrial worker around 1914'.[75] This has for the first time in history somewhat reduced the burden of being a housewife and enabled more women to go out to 'work' outside the home so that they can enjoy more the 'work' they do inside it.

Househusbands have been as absorbed as housewives by the same sort of miniaturizing machines which have brought entertainment out of the collective and into the private domain, starting with the gramophone, continuing through radio, television and videos and perhaps about to be extended still more by cables into the home that will have more channels than men (or women) will know what to do with; and even more by the cars which have largely replaced their ancestors in the tram, the bus and the train, just as in their day these replaced the horse. If the rise in the standard of life of which so much is made has consisted in quite large part in prevailing on consumers to take over work formerly done by paid employees, serving themselves in supermarkets and cafeterias and self-service petrol stations and above all in their homes, they have at least had the aid of the miniature machines which have been the children of the giant machines and giant technology which produced them. The attitude to the miniature machines in the sphere of unpaid work is quite different from that to the large machines of paid work. People become fond of machines whenever they can control them instead of being controlled by them, as they can render biddable the vehicles which have replaced their feet or the little mechanical laundries which have replaced their hands. The love for machines made into slaves is as great as the loathing for machines made into masters. The small machine is beautiful to the new mechanized peasantry of the twentieth century which is almost as intent on its homestead as the medieval peasantry was on its land.

Will the same thing happen to paid work as has already happened to unpaid? The prospects for co-operatives will depend upon it one way or another. If it is not altogether too optimistic a view in an age when gloom is all the fashion, we would answer, yes. The first reason is to do with one of the most fundamental trends in the design of machines. Mechanization has, as its intricacy has developed, always eaten up the less interesting jobs just because the element of human skill in them is also less. If it is a job which can be done by relatively unskilled hands it is at the same time a job which can be taken over by a machine, and as machines have become more skilled, so they have been able to take over more and more jobs done by hand. Now, with the advance of the computer, the same applies to jobs which are thought of as being done by the brain rather more than by the hand, the arm or the feet. Since less skilled jobs are also on the whole more boring, the long-term trend, contrary to a common belief, is to reduce the number of boring jobs. The number of boring jobs being eliminated is over the long term greater than the number of skilled jobs being taken over by machines. The more this happens, the more the most stultifying specialist jobs are removed from industry, and consequently the more commitment there is to work, the better the chance for active participation in the way it is organized.

The second reason for optimism is that these technological changes have been accompanied by others which have favoured the small unit of production as against the large. In the past the very large plant has predominated in industries like steel, chemicals and automobiles and they are of course still important. But one of the reasons for the largeness no longer persists as strongly as it did. Vast numbers of people had to congregate in one space because it aided communication between them, much of which had to be face-to-face. For a colleague to be in the next office or even in the next building is no longer so necessary now that telephones are supported by teleprinters and computers, and indeed it may be much better that he should not be so near. In a small unit management is more independent, workforce morale usually higher, strikes and absenteeism less. Most people know each other personally. This is recognized by many even of the largest organizations. The weight in the economy of the top corporations has continued to grow – they control a larger share of the nation's assets. But the average size of plant in their groups, whether or not these are on the Japanese scale, has been getting smaller and the long-term trend in industry, as in the home, is towards miniaturization of more skilful machines. Information technology also means that more, better and more pointed information can be available at every level in an enterprise, and no longer needs to be so concentrated at the top, or on one site, as it used to be, and often still is.

It may be paradoxical that as the seven-league boots of modern communications have become hundred-league boots they have supported workplaces which have become even smaller in size, even if one does not count the home as a 'workplace'. But it is no less true for being paradoxical. Without that paradox there would, in our view, be very little hope for the economy or the civilization of the Western world. With it, there is some hope that the place where paid work is done will become more like the place where unpaid work is done. Alvin Toffler, looking fifty years ahead, is one who believes we shall see in the USA – and there is no reason why his country should be unique – the growth of an electronic version of the cottage industry of the past and (if we are right in what we have been saying) of the present.

> As mass production wanes and information processing technology is introduced widely, the factory as we know it will disappear. On assembly lines robots will do much of the work. Many employees will no longer go to a centralised place to perform their jobs; instead, they will work at home. Thus the US will see a rise in an electronic version of the cottage industry. This return to the cottage industry (the production method of 200 years ago) has great implications for society and the way people will live. Technology will speed job obsolescence: people will change careers – not just jobs – three or four times in their lifetimes.[76]

Well before fifty years are gone the virtues of smallness in the ordinary workplace should have become a great deal more evident than they are today, even though the small units are grouped with the aid of computers into co-operative networks of the Basque and Japanese sort. This matters so much to co-operative companies because it is almost axiomatic that participatory management will be blocked or at least impeded by bigness. Co-operatives need to be small, with the family being a much more apt model than US Steel or a giant collective farm in the Soviet Union. The view of the Caja is that as a rule co-ops should not have a labour force of more than 500. Above that, members cannot participate in any real sense in the control of their enterprise. The point has been made in this way by the leading modern theorist of co-operatives:

> First, on strictly psychological and sociological grounds, in self-governing bodies which participate in collective income there will be a natural tendency to break into the smallest possible operational units (collectives) consistent with economic efficiency. The simple reason for this is the natural desire not to have men fundamentally remote from one's position participating in decisions and income. Traditional and modern capitalist firms have, by contrast, the well-known tendency to grow without bounds, the interests of the majority of employees being neglected. Very often the capitalist firms will tend to grow even well beyond a size that would be warranted on grounds of efficient operation.[77]

The third reason why work may get more satisfying has to do with changes in the occupational structure. Colin Clark, the well-known economist, long ago put precision into the proposition that 'as time goes on and communities become economically advanced, the numbers engaged in agriculture tend to decline relative to the numbers engaged in manufacture, which in their turn decline relative to the numbers engaged in services'.[78] Domestic service, public transport and shipping have gone down. But these decreases have been more than counterbalanced by the growth of education, health and other social services, by public administration generally, by insurance, banking and finance and by all manner of professional services as well as the new and old communication industries. This change, which has occurred if on different scales in every industrialized country, is due to the faster rise of productivity in manufacturing than outside it and to the fact that people spend a larger proportion of their income upon services and a lower proportion on goods as they get richer.

As a generalization this trend has from our point of view been favourable. A leading American scholar of the subject has put it like this:

> The transfer from a craft society to one of mass production was said to depersonalize work and alienate the worker. The advent of a service economy implies a reversal of these trends. Employees in many service industries are closely related to their work and often engage in a highly personalized activity that offers ample scope for the development and exercise of personal skill . . . It may be true that the initial impact of automation is the substitution of machinery and controls (highly impersonal) for work that was formerly done by human labor. Given full employment, however, the major impact of automation is to eliminate relatively routine, impersonal work entirely, with the result that if one looks at the kind of work people are now doing – the type of work that is growing most rapidly – it is typically of a much more personal character than before.[79]

The same thing has happened even without full employment. The entry of so many new co-operatives into service industries – wholesaling, computer programming, printing, cleaning and the rest – is therefore something to be welcomed. Industry is no longer industry in the old-fashioned sense of the word.

So these two trends are not unfavourable. They may be making paid work more absorbing rather than less. But the crucial factor is not mechanization even when it has the microchip added to it or the switch in the occupational structure away from manufacturing. It is the degree to which there can be some escape from the hold of organizational bureaucracy. Increasing mechanization may have added directly to human satisfaction; it is much more doubtful whether the equally tenacious trend towards increasing bureaucratization has done so. As the division of labour has steadily expanded on a world scale, with Japanese videos in the backstreets of Birmingham, Scotch whisky on sale in all the supermarkets of Bangkok, and a Mercedes in the garage of every self-regarding African politician, so has the world economy become more impersonal. Even small organizations are caught up in this same universe with all its cross-cutting channels of trade and communication. The transactions are not between one person and another, but between one organization and another; and within any large organization, or even sometimes in medium-sized ones, the relationships are more between the holders of offices than between people. The offices have a certain durability to them irrespective of who is holding them: it is not so much a person as the managing director (whoever he happens to be) who communicates with the works manager, the foreman with the operator, the office manager with the receptionist. If one job-holder goes, another comes to occupy the same slot. The job is dead; long live the office.

If this were not so, the economic system might not have held up even as well as it has. When work is inherently fulfilling, people are only too happy to do it. They clamour for jobs of quality. But work has been boring for so many during the long transition period when they have been turned into a species of human machine, before their work has been taken over by real machines. Such work is unpleasant to do except for those who can avoid it by living in a fantasy world of their own while they are going through the motions demanded of them. If it is unpleasant, it will only be done under discipline and management has had – one might say has had to have – the power of duress in order to get the world's work done at all when the world's work is so unsatisfying to perform. The power has remained not so much because of anything that has happened at work as because of all the changes outside work to which we have been referring, coupled in recent years with the prevalence of unemployment which has made dismissal a much worse punishment than it was. If the real life is outside work, and if the enjoyment of that life depends upon money, the power of management resides in its ability to sack people and deprive them of the money to spend on maintaining the state of life to which the miniaturization of technology has called them; and in its ability to promote people so that they share a little of the power residing in the Praetorian Guard of management and also have more of the money which they think they need to assert themselves when not on duty. Another factor is that any management with confidence in its own right to give orders is also always buttressed by the people who actually like to receive orders – the subordinates who feel more secure when they are servants than when they are masters. There is as much of the slave in all of us as there is of the master.

But as power in one bureaucracy has increased, the drive for personal autonomy has gathered momentum. The proportion of people content to be servants, of a bureaucracy or of another individual person, has fallen away. Without recognizing the value placed on the desirability of personal autonomy the nature of modern civilization can hardly be understood at all. Autonomy is only another word for liberty – the liberty of individual people to decide for themselves what they shall do and not do. The hope of enhancing that autonomy or liberty has been behind almost all the changes fought for over the centuries in the political sphere. Those who demand equality have for the most part only been seeking the extension of the same liberties to all and objecting to some of them being reserved for a minority. The movement has on the whole been remarkably successful, and accounts for the degree of consensus that exists about the way a government should be selected. The parties – including the SDP of course – are competing for power. But the proper procedure for resolving that competition is accepted by all. The electors are to arbitrate. The parties are also less divided on class lines than they were. The bitterness of the class struggle is now in evidence not so much in politics as in industry.

Whether that bitterness can be overcome will, to sum up so far in this chapter, depend in part upon whether we are right about the cumulative effect of the changes we have been itemizing. We have suggested that paid work will become more satisfying – more like unpaid work in fact. The great trade-off would then be a much less prominent social device. There could then be some refocusing of interest on the workplace, so that paid work was not so much a means to private ends. Then at least one of the necessary preconditions could be met for a more active democracy at work and for a much wider acceptance of responsibility for the common concerns of people at work. The workers might become less indifferent than Michels believed they will always be, especially in small co-operatives built to a human scale.

Attitudes of unions

But this is not, of course, to say it will happen, only that it could. Whether it does will turn as much as anything on the attitudes of first, trade unions, and then, management, to participation in industry. We will deal with the unions first.

We said in Chapter 2 that when the trade unions gradually became the dominant working-class institution they eclipsed the co-operatives and the rest. In industry the unions have continued to assert that workers, even though subordinate in an industrial hierarchy, should have the same rights to self-determination as anyone else. This they have done in their characteristic way, not by demanding that trade unionists should take part in management but, while accepting that management has general responsibility for administering the business in question, or the office, public service, or civil service department, doing their best to limit the exercise of that power by ensuring that it does not bear too heavily on individual workers and, of course, to push up the wages of their members so that they will have the more opportunity to do their own thing in their unpaid work. The divide between management and unions has been bitter because so much is at stake on both sides.

The balance of power was swung towards the unions by the full employment that lasted for over twenty years after the war, the power of management to sack people being blunted when anyone dismissed could so easily get another job elsewhere and could not so easily be replaced. The power of the unions to raise the wages of their members was also increased and there was nothing to stop them from pushing the increases above the gains in productivity, a matter that became increasingly serious when productivity increases began to slow down so markedly after the oil cartel came into existence. The root problem for the country, and in the long run for the unions themselves, is that the extra power they gained was of a negative rather than a positive kind. They attacked management without accepting much responsibility themselves for the quantity or quality of production. They wanted more without helping to create more.

The Thatcher Government has had only one counter to

propose and one to act on, which was to undo the post-war economic settlement and increase not employment but unemployment. The hope was that the balance of power would be shifted back to management and more discipline restored as a result. The hope has not been completely disappointed, though at a high cost in human misery. But in the long run such an attempt is in our view doomed to fail, and could bring down political democracy into the bargain. In that event genuine trade unions will themselves disappear, as they did in both fascist and communist countries. Inside a political democracy, whose rationale is to give expression to the basic need for human autonomy, the house cannot indefinitely be divided against itself, with the basic need being recognized in politics but not in industry. The principle cannot, without intolerable stress, be honoured in one sphere and dishonoured in another.

But the unions have not led the attack on the autocratic management which too often rejects the claim to autonomy. They even seem to be committed to the maintenance of a style of management which invites and gets opposition. The Labour Party does not want to reform the House of Lords because as long as the Lords' constitution is indefensible (which it is) it can be attacked root and branch. So it is with management. As long as it is in effect accountable to no one but itself – the 'owners' having slid into obscurity – the trade unions can attack it without let or hindrance, ranting the while about their own superiority in this regard. Union leaders are at any rate nominally and often in practice accountable to their members. They at least have been influenced enough by the value of autonomy to model their constitutions on Parliament itself. The unions too have elections, for their officers and governing bodies, and it is notable that many of their critics in all parties, while not recognizing the case for applying the same principles to the management side of industry, do not question the need for democracy in the unions but only its incompleteness. They want to make unions even more akin to Parliament by encouraging or making compulsory secret ballots and postal ballots which will enable many more of the members to vote than do so at the moment, except in unions which are already following these practices.

But few have taken that vital further step and sought to make managerial leadership as accountable as union leadership. Many unionists hoped as a result of nationalization to do this for whole industries at once. Unions are never, or hardly ever, organized on the basis of one company – those that used to be were called 'company unions' and derided for being the employer's creature. If not industrial unions, like the miners, the steel-workers, the textile or the boot- and shoe-workers, they are general unions which cover many industries. The appeal is always to a more general class or to industrial solidarity which goes far wider than any one company, and is indeed intended to pose an alternative to any loyalty there might be to an individual employer. The solidarity has the great advantage of going so wide, sometimes extending well beyond Britain; there is nothing parochial about it. Many union leaders hoped that an industry-wide solidarity would, once there was nationalization, lead to all those em-ployed working for each and each for all. Unfortunately this has not been the outcome. The solidarity has been mobi-lized against the management quite as effectively as it has in privately-owned industry. Nor is management accountability any greater.

If the route of nationalization has proved a dead end, it should re-open once again the whole question of workers' control. Public ownership, post-war style, is not the only sort of common ownership; and it was certainly not always seen as such. The official Objects of the Amalgamated Union of Engineering Workers include 'the control of industry in the interests of the community . . . the extension of co-operative production to assist in altering the competitive system of society for a co-operative system'. The Objects of the Transport and General Workers' Union refer to 'the extension of co-operative production and distribution . . . the securing of a real measure of control in industry and participation by the workers in the management, in the interests of labour and the general community'. The Electrical, Telecommunications and Plumbing Union wants 'by legal means and the supporting of legislative action to elevate the moral, intellectual and social conditions of all workers by supporting policies which will ultimately give the workers ownership and control of industry'.[80]

Workers' control used to mean participation by the workers

in the management; it could do so again. If it did, the units of organization would have to be much smaller than in the nationalized industries. They were all taken into public ownership when belief in the economies (rather than the diseconomies) of scale was still very much in fashion. With smaller units the workers could own *and* control. This would mean dividing the industries into smaller units and gradually transferring the ownership to the people who work in them.

Any return to these original objects would also be an important departure from present practice. The workers through their unions oppose the management; they do not take part in it, for fear of compromising and dividing themselves. Being in opposition, as long as it is permanent opposition with never the possibility of becoming the 'government', does confer a kind of strength. The orthodoxy was described by Clegg.

> The trade union cannot become the organ of industrial management; there would be no one to oppose the management, and no hope of democracy. Nor can the union enter into an unholy alliance for the joint management of industry, for its opposition functions would then become subordinate and finally stifled.[81]

But on this matter the orthodoxy does not seem as sacrosanct as it did. There is a movement away from it in the regions if not so much at the centre. The Scottish TUC was, as we noted earlier, one of the originators of SCDC. The Wales TUC has taken a more dramatic step. It sent a delegation to Mondragon and was so impressed that it determined to try and create a Welsh counterpart. This is to run an information service on co-ops, prepare planning, marketing and feasibility studies, provide practical assistance to all associated co-operatives, train managers and other staff, find people with particular skills not available locally, and give legal and other advice.[82] In November 1982 the Secretary of State for Wales announced a grant of £100,000 spread over three years to help set up the Wales Co-operative Development Centre and a similar amount is expected from the EEC. The hope is also to establish a worker savings and investment scheme which could in time become a smaller version of the Caja.

Meanwhile, the Transport and General Workers' Union, in

particular, has shown how valuable trade-union support can be for new and struggling co-operatives. Under its auspices three clothing co-operatives in Wales and in Taunton have been brought together into a small grouping of the kind that we have already appealed for several times. Led by Moss Evans, the union's officers have spent time advising the co-operatives and given them union orders for their goods as well as helping to secure other orders for them. British unions have not gone as far as Italian ones which have imposed a levy of 0.5 per cent on members' wages in order to build up a fund for financing co-operatives and so providing more jobs for their members, or as the Danish trade unions which have supplied capital for many worker co-ops. But they are perhaps on the way.

The Welsh initiative has provoked a new debate about the role of unions in a co-operative. No one, or hardly anyone, has suggested that co-operatives can come into existence without accepting flexibility in wages and the elimination of work practices which can no longer be tolerated once workers are in control. For all that, experience has demonstrated that unions are still needed. It is apparent that unions should separate their representative functions from their involvement in managerial decisions.

Denis Gregory has drawn an analogy with the fashioning of roles for shop stewards who, under the Health and Safety at Work Act, have become safety representatives as well, with certain quasi-executive functions to perform.

The potential conflict of interests visited upon the shop steward, who is also a safety representative, has long been recognised. However, by dint of considerable education and training efforts, shop steward structures in well organised workplaces appear to allow safety representatives to operate alongside of conventional shop steward functions. The most successful systems are those whereby the stewards have had the confidence to recognise that safety representatives need to 'distance' themselves from many of the day-to-day concerns of the steward in order to develop specific health and safety skills and to avoid uncritical compromises. In this way, some separation of orthodox representational functions from a more technically specific role can be achieved which does not appear to erode the overall effectiveness of the shop steward organisation.[83]

The same separation of roles could allow shop stewards to continue to represent their individual members as well as taking part in management. Democracy does not need to work through a single channel and indeed cannot unless it is to be stultified. The unions could be particularly needed in a co-operative to protect the interests of individual members against the majority. A majority is always in danger of becoming a tyrant.

Attitudes of managers

The prospects turn not just on unions, but on management. There is perhaps a certain sense to what has happened in management. Many jobs have been so boring, so repetitious that they might hardly have been done at all in the absence of effective and imposed discipline at work. This is all the more the case because work has over the last century come to be organized on such a large scale as to bear heavily on man's spirit. It is difficult to feel a person inside a large organization. The inevitable protests at the loss of human dignity seem to require managers who have strong enough powers to hold the protests in check.

Given all the changes in society generally which have detracted from the unthinking acceptance of authority, it is remarkable that managers have retained as much power as they have. They have only done so because they have enjoyed two particular advantages. When there have been many shareholders they have not in practice been accountable to anyone for the power they wield. But few people are content to be so much on their own as that. They do not want to appear autocrats even if they are, or perhaps especially when they are. But they can muster the courage to behave autocratically all the same as long as they appear to be accountable even if it is only to dummies. Managers *appear* to be accountable to shareholders and many of them consider that is how things are. Shareholders want the maximum profits and managers consider that by doing their best to satisfy that want they are demonstrating their accountability. Managers can always claim that they are no more personally responsible than the soldier who carries out distasteful orders which come from on high.

But this concentration of power, however necessary it may once have been, has precipitated the crisis of modern capitalism, or perhaps one should say modern managerialism, since capitalists as such have to a large extent been superseded by managers. Workers deprived of any share in management have turned instead to strengthen trade unions and these have been driven into permanent opposition and have grown so resolute in their negative stance that dealing with them takes up an inordinate amount of managerial time, just as dealing with the inflationary effects of their actions takes up an inordinate amount of the time of governments. The unions have been forced into, as well as willing on themselves, the position of having power without responsibility.

Is there any other way of changing the situation in its fundamentals except by making managers accountable to the employees? We hardly need to state our point of view again. We do not see any solution except by changing the status of workers, from that of employees into that of partners. The two estates would then no longer be locked in conflict. If they so remain, they could between them destroy the civilization of which they have been part. In a totalitarian system trade unions are forced to abandon their opposition and everyone's liberty suffers in consequence. In a democratic system they will, if all goes well, be persuaded to do so and to take up new roles in a new kind of industrial democracy which will also complement and preserve political democracy. There is no longer any future in the discipline which is exercised over unwilling people by managements who are none too assured despite the advantages we have cited. In an age when jobs are slowly becoming more interesting (and scarcer) the only good prospects in a democracy are for a greater measure of self-discipline and for authority exercised with the consent of those to whom it is accountable. Our hope is that more and more managers, and young would-be managers, will recognize the force of the appeal and welcome the prospect of working in a much less tense, more harmonious setting.

Conclusion

The characteristic mood of our times is gloom. Few people expect any new harmony to prevail at the dawn of the next millennium; the much commoner view is that the world itself will end before the end of our present millennium, or if the cataclysm is avoided more by good luck than by good judgement, society will peter down into ever more discord within nations and between nations, with people ever more divided by the demon of a jealous competition.

But there is no necessity for this to happen. There could be a new moral attitude to human relations in industry. The Pope recently put it like this:

> We must emphasize and give prominence to the primacy of man in the production process, the primacy of man over things. Everything contained in the concept of capital in the strict sense is only a collection of things. Man, as the subject of work, and independently of the work that he does – man alone is a person.[84]

More people may actually be guided by such principles in the conduct of their working lives. There may even be a general return to more spiritual values.

To justify such optimism we have to do again what we have done before in this chapter and indeed earlier in the book, and prop ourselves up against the past. According to our interpretation, the Industrial Revolution brought about a sharp separation between work and leisure. Before that, most people lived on and off the land, doing backbreaking work, it is true, and often in miserable conditions. But the day was lived through without any distinction being made between these two halves of life. Work, when doing it drew in full measure upon the skills and talents a person had, produced the satisfaction that has in more modern times been reserved for leisure. Work was performed inside the family, acting as a collective for the purpose of production. Men and women did not go out to work, or children out to school, and then come home for leisure. They stayed and worked at home, or in the fields nearby, and such leisure as they had, where the term was even conceived of, was also for the most part enjoyed or borne with in the same domestic setting.

Since then the course of industrialization, and now de-indus-trialization, has carried the family through different stages of development, first into towns where few except for the 'leisured classes' had either time to spare after the long and gruelling hours of work or amenities to repair to if there had been time; and then, eventually, to the stage where the split between work and leisure was necessary to the maintenance of the economic order. People were, and are, sufficiently obedient to authority to allow the economy to survive because authority controls access to the real life in leisure. This real life has become increasingly like an updated and mechanized version of family life before industrialization, with skills being drawn on for the domestic crafts and for growing things, and talents being used for the cultivation of beauty around them as people conceive beauty to be.

In our view we are only extrapolating from what already appears to be happening. The home is already the workshop wherever the structure of the family has stood up to the winds of change. The only difference we see is that in an electronic age this workshop, organized as it usually is as a very informal co-operative, will not continue to produce goods and services only for domestic consumption but, increasingly, will do so as well for sale outside the home.

As for paid work of the more ordinary sort, we can only say again that we envisage it becoming more like domestic production, if on a larger scale, with such a reconciliation between work and leisure that the separation between them will be replaced by a unification. Burke said that the most singular characteristic of the family is that it admirably reconciles altruism with selfishness. But as society has evolved, the altruism, and the commitment, have been reserved for the family as the domestic unit both of consumption and production, while the selfishness has found its expression in paid work. In the new dispensation the two inclinations, allied as they are to the pair we contrasted with each other in Chapter 2, co-operation and competition, could be blended with each other in new ways. There could be a little more emphasis in paid as well as unpaid work upon altruism and co-operation.

This book has been largely concerned with means, the means of organizing industry on a new pattern and the means of creating co-operative companies which might be able to overcome the Webb weaknesses. Some of the new approaches we have been suggesting are for government and some for existing voluntary bodies to consider if they see fit to do so. We could not leave out the agencies already operating in the field because, unless in tune with them, the policy of any government would be without any proper context.

The non-governmental institution which matters most, and to which we have referred time and time again, is that of the unions. Some of them have given support for the kind of modest growth there has been so far. But we are hoping for much more than that: a far-reaching change of attitude which could produce, say, an extra one million jobs in co-operatives before 1990. This would mean pulling back from their alliance with the state and their commitment to nationalization as the *only* hallowed form of public ownership. If they changed that attitude and considered what they could do on their own, it would indeed be a watershed for the unions and for the country and perhaps other countries as well. Workers' control in a new form would be back on the union, and hence on the political, agenda.

We are asking, we are hoping, for a great deal, not just for the unions but for the role which co-operatives could play in bringing about a revolution from within our society. They are starting off from a low base in an economy and in a culture which does not favour them. While they are in such a minority position they have to conform to the dominant values and the dominant institutions of our time. These have encouraged most people to adopt an individualist, self-regarding style in their lives, and co-operatives cannot for the moment ignore the prevailing mood. But in time they could become much more of a force and as they did they could, with their own new institutions in support, reach the critical mass which would allow them to build up a partially independent culture which stood out from the general. They could help to create a new way of life which would eventually and by slow degrees engender new values in the whole of society.

There will be a better chance of this happening if it is recognized by all those engaged in the debate that the steps we have been discussing, even the new approach which may yet be adopted by the unions, are all means to ends.[85] The purpose of co-operatives is not just to run successful businesses, though successful of their kind they have to be, but to elevate the dignity of labour; to give more choice about how work should be done; to make paid work more fun; to give a new sense of independence to people who have always been told what to do; to release the creative talents and imagination which bureaucracy has suppressed; to convert conflict in industry into a friendly partnership between management and members; to make work into a school for cultivation of people's sympathies for each other; and to bring out more altruism by giving more opportunity for it to be expressed.

Appendix
Checkpoints for would-be co-operators

Introduction

As we mentioned in Chapter 4, people have many different motives for starting co-operatives. For some the main one will be to save jobs; for others it will be to keep a firm going when its owner dies or retires and there is no obvious successor. But the majority of new co-operatives fall into neither of these categories: they are started from scratch. Many more of them are needed. This guide is primarily for people who are thinking of setting up a brand new co-operative business. We stress again as we did in Chapter 5 that high ideals and a commitment to the co-operative way of working are not in themselves enough to make new co-ops survive. They have to be efficient businesses as well as places in which people can work together more harmoniously than usual. We cannot pretend to tell people everything they need to know to set up a successful co-operative – so much depends on circumstances. All we can do is consider some of the things you'll need to do and suggest people and organizations who may be able to help you. The facts and figures are, as far as we know, correct at the time of going to press. We identify five decisions that must be taken, or problems that must be solved.

The first is which type of co-op to set up. The second is to work out a business plan. The third is to get additional training if it is needed. The fourth is to find suitable premises. Finally, there is the crucial question of how to go about raising the finance.

1 Which type of co-op to go for?

There are plenty to choose from. A co-operative can be set up either as a society under the Industrial and Provident Societies Acts or as a company under the Companies Acts and must in both cases satisfy the relevant Registrar (whose address is given at the end of this section) that it meets all the regulations laid down by law. It is also possible to set up as a partnership, in which case you don't have to register with anyone, but the partnership form has the strong disadvantage that the members of the co-op will be personally liable for any debts incurred by it and could as a result lose any personal property they have got. For that reason we shall concentrate here on the other two forms, company and society. Whichever you go for it will probably be quicker and cheaper to use a set of model rules provided by one of the support organizations we discussed in Chapter 5. The main ones are as follows.

Industrial and Common Ownership Movement

ICOM offers two sets of model rules, one for an industrial and provident society, the other for a company limited by guarantee. As we have seen, ICOM belongs to the collectivist school and this is reflected in the rules they offer. The key features of both sets are that only workers of the co-operative can be members; that members can hold only one £1 share in the co-operative (although they may put up capital themselves by way of loans); and that if the co-operative is dissolved, any residual assets may not be shared out between members but must be transferred to a common ownership enterprise or central fund or used for charitable purposes. The ICOM model rules make no mention of a manager but provide for a committee to be elected by all the members on the basis of one member, one vote. It is this committee which is legally responsible for managing all aspects of running the co-op which are not the responsibility of the general meeting of all members. Any committee member may be removed from office by a majority vote at a general meeting. The general meeting also decides the proportion of any profits which will be used to add to the co-operative's reserves, as a bonus to members or for some social or charitable purpose.

153

The company form is especially useful for new co-ops with fewer than seven members (the minimum necessary for registration under the Industrial and Provident Societies Acts). By the end of 1981, the year ICOM introduced the company model rules, 40 per cent of new registrations were using that form. To use either set of rules a co-operative must also subscribe to ICOM and thereafter will, of course, be entitled to play a part in the running of ICOM itself. The work of actually registering the new co-operative is done by ICOM staff. In April 1983 the cost of registration (including subscription to ICOM) was £185 for the company form and £195 for the Industrial and Provident Society.

Co-operative Development Agency

The CDA produced a new set of model rules for co-operatives in 1982, using the Industrial and Provident Societies Acts. They are intended to provide an alternative to those of ICOM for co-operators who want to have a personal stake in their co-operative in the form of share capital. The CDA rules supersede those of the old Co-operative Productive Federation on which they are based. The key features are that the co-operatives can have outside members (who may be individuals or corporate bodies such as trade unions or retail societies, although of course no member can have more than one vote); members may put in share capital up to the legal limit of £10,000 per member; and it is left to the members to decide what should happen to the assets of the co-operative if it is dissolved. The CDA rules specifically allow for the appointment of a manager by the committee elected by the general meeting of all the members. The manager is answerable both to the committee and to the membership as a whole. Profits can be applied in the following ways:

a) to a general reserve;
b) as a bonus to members in proportion to their earnings;
c) to pay up to 5 per cent interest on shareholdings;
d) as a bonus to members in the form of shares in proportion to any increase in the value of the assets of the co-operative in the previous year;
e) for social or charitable purposes.

Registration is done by CDA staff and costs £105 (which is the fee charged by the Registrar of Friendly Societies) plus £5 handling fee. The CDA does not have members, so there is no sub-scription charge as there is with ICOM.

Job Ownership Limited

Unlike any of the models provided by ICOM or the CDA, Job Ownership co-operatives take the form of companies limited by shares. As with the CDA (but not ICOM), individual members are encouraged to hold substantial capital stakes and, as with ICOM (but not the CDA), only workers may be members.

Other distinctive features are that shares in a Job Ownership Company cannot be freely bought and sold as they can in a traditional company limited by shares; the value of an indivi-dual's share varies according to the length of service and the contribution to the work of the company by the person con-cerned; there is provision for collectively owned 'A' shares (con-stituting around 20 per cent of the company's total share capital) and individually owned 'B' shares (constituting the other 80 per cent). The capital represented by the 'A' shares may be used by the company to buy back the 'B' shares when a worker leaves or retires. 'A' shareholders can never benefit personally from their shareholding even in the event that the company is dissolved. But a 'B' shareholder can expect to get back the value of his share plus a sum which reflects the growth in value of the company's assets since he joined. There is, as yet, no set fee for using the JOL model constitution. The registration fee for a company is £50.

Scottish Co-operatives Development Committee

For new co-ops setting up in Scotland, SCDC offers a set of model rules very similar to those of ICOM for a company limited by guarantee. The fee is just the £50 payable to the Registrar of Companies since SCDC does not charge for its services.

Local Co-operative Development Agencies

Advice on which set of rules will be best for you could be on your doorstep. Nearly sixty local CDAs are listed in the *Directory of Industrial and Service Co-operatives* published by the national CDA in the autumn of 1982 (price £6.90). They should all be able to offer guidance on the type of constitution to adopt. Many themselves produce a guide to starting a worker co-op. If there isn't a CDA near where you live, you should write direct to any or all of the organizations listed below.

Useful addresses

Industrial Common Ownership Movement
7/8 The Corn Exchange
Leeds LS1 7BP
Tel: 0532 461737

Co-operative Development Agency
20 Albert Embankment
London SE1 7TJ
Tel: 01-211 6097

Job Ownership Limited
9 Poland Street
London W1V 3DG
Tel: 01-437 5511

Scottish Co-operatives Development Committee Ltd
Templeton Business Centre
Templeton Street
Bridgeton
Glasgow G40 1DA
Tel: 041-554 3797

The Registrar of Friendly Societies
17 North Audley Street
London W1Y 2AP
Tel: 01-629 7001

The Registrar of Companies
Companies Registration Office
Crown Way
Maindy, Cardiff CF4 3UZ
Tel: 0222 388588

Useful publications

Roger Sawtell and Michael Campbell, *A Guide to the ICOM Model Rules* (Industrial Common Ownership Movement)

How to form an Industrial Co-operative: Folder containing copies of ICOM model rules and all the forms required to register an ICOM co-operative. Available from Industrial Common Ownership Movement. Leaflets are also available on such topics as *Disciplinary Procedure in Common Ownerships*

Campbell B. Burns, *Co-operative Law* (Education Department, Co-operative Union Limited, Stanford Hall, Loughborough)

Peter Cockerton, Tim Gilmour-White, John Pearce, Anna Whyatt, *Workers' Co-operatives: A Handbook* (Aberdeen People's Press)

David H. Wright, *Co-operative and Community: The Theory and Practice of Producer Co-operatives* (Bedford Square Press)

John Fryer, *Legal Structures for Co-operatives* (Beechwood College, Leeds)

Jim Brown, *How to start a Workers' Co-operative* (Beechwood College)

2 Preparing a business plan

Perhaps one of the biggest problems facing a new co-op (or indeed, any other new small business) is that it will by definition have no track record with which to convince potential financiers. Members of the co-op often haven't got very much capital of their own to put up so they need outside money. It will be vital to prepare a sound business plan to show banks and others that you know just what you are doing. This might include:

a) a detailed description of the product or service that you are planning to sell and what will make it better (or cheaper) than similar products or services already on the market. The competition needs to be described and sized up;

b) definition of the market you are aiming at, the way you propose to reach it and details of any customers already lined up;

c) whether you have taken any steps to safeguard your position by obtaining a patent or registering your business name;

d) descriptions of the people who are going to work in the co-operative and their experience and skills as well as information about their financial commitment to it; whether members are willing (or able) to offer security or guarantees to offset the risk to the lender;

e) what the management structure is going to be; whether day-to-day decision-making will be delegated to a manager or whether such decisions will be made collectively;

f) information about premises; how much capital will be needed to buy or convert and equip them and details of the terms of any lease agreements especially if personal guarantees have been sought from members;

g) how much money is needed for investment in fixed assets such as machinery and equipment and how much is needed for working capital for holding stocks, paying initial wages, giving credit to customers and other purposes. You will need to produce a detailed cash flow forecast showing all income and expenditure in each month in which you expect to incur it. This should be done in fine detail for the first year at least and as a broad estimation for the next few years as well. Whoever is going to supply money will want to know that the co-operative will be able to service all its loans and that you have allowed for the likely impact of inflation on costs and selling prices.

Help in drawing up a business plan can be got from a variety of sources. Start with your local CDA, if there is one, because the people there will be familiar with the problems that are peculiar to co-operatives and may also have valuable contacts with local bank managers and other financiers. If you are opting for an ICOM constitution it would be worth getting in touch with them to find out whether there are any individual members living near you who have some special skills to offer in accountancy, law etc.

Another useful source of help could be the Department of Industry's Small Firms Service which gives information and literature as well as business counselling. A small fee is charged after an initial consultation which is free. Similar services are offered in Scotland, Wales and Northern Ireland through the Scottish and Welsh Development Agencies and the Local Enterprise Development Unit respectively.

Yet another source of help could be one of the Local Enterprise Trusts which have been set up in many parts of the country. In London, the London Enterprise Agency offers free advice on finance, marketing and premises and the recently set up Greater London Enterprise Board offers loans or grants specifically for feasibility studies for new co-operatives, in addition to a variety of other services. If your co-op is being set up in a rural area then another source of help would be the Council for Small Industries in Rural Areas whose staff give advice on marketing and managing. COSIRA is based at Salisbury but has offices in most counties.

Useful addresses
For local CDAs consult the *Directory of Industrial and Service Co-operatives* mentioned above or ask at your local Town Hall. The Employment Division or the Planning Department of the local authority should be able to tell you if a local CDA has recently been set up.

Department of Industry
Small Firms Service
123 Victoria Street
London SW1
Tel: 01-212 5492
(or dial 100 and ask for Freefone 2444 to get your local Small Firms Centre)

Scottish Development Agency
120 Bothwell Street
Glasgow G2 7JP
Tel: 041-248 2700

Welsh Development Agency
Treforest Industrial Estate
Pontypridd
Mid Glamorgan CF37 5UT
Tel: 044-385 2666

Local Enterprise Development Unit
Lamont House
Purdy's Lane
Newtownbreda
Belfast BT8 4TB
Tel: 0232 691031

Local Enterprise Trusts
(A list of addresses of Trusts is given in *Raising Finance*, by Clive Woodcock - see below.)

London Enterprise Agency
69 Cannon Street
London EC4
Tel: 01-236 2676

Greater London Enterprise Board
63-67 Newington Causeway
London SE1
Tel: 01-403 0300

Council for Small Industries in Rural Areas
141 Castle Street
Salisbury
Wiltshire
Tel: 0722 6255

Useful publications

Clive Woodcock, *Raising Finance: The Guardian Guide for the Small Business* (Kogan Page)

Be Your Own Boss Kit, from the National Extension College, 18 Brooklands Avenue, Cambridge (£5.95 excluding postage)

Micheline Mason, *Creating Your Own Work* (Gresham Books)

Tolley's Survival Kit for Small Businesses (Tolley Publishing)

The *Guardian* devotes a section to small businesses every Friday

Titled Sources of Information for New and Small Businesses, from the Small Business Unit, Thames Polytechnic School of Business Administration, Riverside House, London SE18 (£1.35 including postage)

3 Training

The training needs of people setting up new co-operatives fall into three main categories. People may need to improve their technical skills, their managerial skills or their co-operative skills. There are a number of ways in which you can go about it. To start with the most general category - technical skills - you are almost certain to find help locally. Ask at your library for a list of the local technical colleges and Adult or Further Education centres and find out what courses are on offer. The Small Firms Service should also be able to advise about courses in basic technical skills.

For advice about courses designed to increase managerial skills, start with your local polytechnic. Or you might consider applying to go on the New Enterprise Programme sponsored by the Manpower Services Commission. The programme is designed to help people setting up new small businesses (including co-operatives) and begins with a four-week residential period during which participants study accounting and financial controls, marketing and pricing policy and employment law. Participants are expected to put up an idea for a new business and in a subsequent twelve-week period they go out to put their idea into practice with the back-up of tutors. At present the New Enterprise Programme is run from four major business schools which are listed below. No formal qualifications are needed and all fees and residential costs as well as a weekly maintenance allowance are paid for by the MSC.

One method of acquiring management skills which is particularly appropriate for people in co-operatives is distance learning. Rather than pay out fees for just one member to attend a course away from the co-op, all the members can participate in a correspondence course and develop their ideas together. We have already mentioned the National Extension College's *Be Your Own Boss Kit*. A correspondence course based on the book is also available and has the added advantage of an NEC tutor to give guidance and advice on following the course. It takes about fourteen weeks to cover and costs around £32.

The main centre for training in co-operatives (as distinct from ordinary businesses) is Beechwood College in Leeds. They run regular three-day courses on how to start a co-operative, how to run one and how to cope with expansion. They also organize seminars on special subjects such as how architects can set up co-operatives, the role of trade unions in co-ops and how a co-op can measure the achievement of its social as opposed to its financial objectives. Costs range from £12 for a one-day course to £77 for a three-day residential course. Beechwood stresses the need for group learning on practical and technical issues.

Other co-operative training centres include Commonwork in Kent, which arranges courses and workshops for people in co-ops, including some tailor-made courses; and the Co-operative College in Loughborough, which puts on a variety of courses for managers in consumer and other co-operatives.

Useful addresses
New Enterprise Programme Centres:

Manchester Business School
Write to: Manpower Services Commission
Training Services Division
Boulton House
17/21 Charlton Street
Manchester MI 3HY

Durham University Business School
Write to: Manpower Services Commission
Training Services Division
Lynus House
Frederick Street
Sunderland
Tyne and Wear SRI ILQ

London Business School
Write to: Manpower Services Commission
Training Services Division
213 Oxford Street
London WI

Scottish Business School
Write to: Manpower Services Commission
Training Services Division
20 Waterloo Street
Glasgow G2 6DT

Other training centres:
National Extension College
18 Brooklands Avenue
Cambridge
Tel: 0223 316644

Beechwood College
Elmete Lane
Roundhay
Leeds LS8 2LQ
Tel: 0532 720205

Commonwork Trust
Bore Place
Bough Beech
Edenbridge
Kent TN8 7AR
Tel: 0732 77255

Co-operative College
Stanford Hall
Loughborough
Leics LE12 5QR
Tel: 050-982 2333

The Plunkett Foundation for Co-operative Studies
31 St Giles
Oxford OX1 3LF
Tel: 0865 53960

Co-operatives Research Unit
Open University
Walton Hall
Milton Keynes MK7 6AA
Tel: 0908 74066

Useful publications

Jim Brown, *Basic Employment Rights in a Workers' Co-operative* (Beechwood College)

Tony McNaughton, *Business Management for Co-operatives and Community Enterprises* (Beechwood College)

Maggi McCormick, *The Complete Guide to Managing Your Own Business* (Eaglemoss Publications)

4 Premises

The first question to ask is whether you need premises at all to start with. Could you use your own or another member's house or garage and save money, at least in the early stages? If not, the next step is to see whether there are any purpose-built or renovated premises which have been designed especially with new small businesses in mind. Increasing numbers are, so check with your local authority or Small Firms Centre for information. Some local CDAs have also gone into the provision of small 'seedbed' workshops for new co-ops and should be one of the first ports of call. Local authorities often keep a list of vacant industrial premises and it is always worth getting that as well as getting on to the lists of local estate agents.

Before you commit yourself to buying or leasing premises there are quite a few questions which you should ask. These include:

1 Will you need to apply for permission for a change of use of the premises? The planning department of the local authority will tell you this. You should also check carefully that the use you want to make of the premises will not infringe any of the health and safety or fire regulations. The Health and Safety Officer and the Fire Officer will both give free advice about changes you may have to make or equipment you may have to buy. It is worth seeking it because both have the power to order the closure of a workplace if there are serious safety risks.

2 What state is the building in and how much will it cost to convert it for your purposes? Consider employing a surveyor to carry out a full structural survey. If there are problems, say with the roof or dry rot, whose responsibility will it be to put them right? If it would be the co-op's responsibility you might be able to negotiate a rent-free period to cover the cost of such repairs. Check, too, whether there are any grants available from the local authority.

3 What are the terms of the lease? Will individual members of the co-operative be expected to give personal guarantees? What will happen if you have to leave the premises before the period of the lease has expired? How wide is the clause which

specifies what the premises may be used for? Does it allow for all the things the co-operative may want to do? It is always wise to get a lease checked by your solicitor before you agree to it. Many local CDAs have solicitors on their staff. If they haven't they should be able to recommend one who is sympathetic and will not charge too much.

5 Raising the finance

Financing new businesses is risky. The financier's aim will be to minimize the risks and to get the highest possible return on his money. The conventional method of doing this is to take an equity stake in the business, which means having a share in the ownership and control as well as a share in the profits. Co-operatives are by definition excluded from raising finance in this way and so it is often more difficult as well as more expensive for them to get the capital they need to start. As a general rule, the more money of your own you can put in, the easier it will be to attract outside finance. Indeed, many financing institutions will not even consider lending unless they can see evidence of a firm financial commitment on the part of the people starting up a new business. How you put the money in will depend on the type of co-op you are starting as well as your personal circumstances. In an ICOM co-op members' investment takes the form of loans; in a co-op set up with CDA or JOL model rules it is possible for members to have substantial shareholdings. If members have not got cash to put into their co-op they may consider raising a loan using personal assets such as a house for security or they may contribute capital by way of regular deduction from wages once the co-op has got going. Having raised as much money as you possibly can of your own and having prepared your business plan along the lines discussed above, the next step will be to shop around. There are a great variety of schemes on offer which cater for co-ops along with other small businesses, some of which we describe here.

The Co-operative Bank is an obvious starting point. The Bank estimates that it already has the accounts of more than half the existing worker co-ops and it is keen to have more. In 1978 the

Bank launched a special scheme whereby it would match pound for pound the investment of members in viable co-ops. It was also among the first banks to participate in the Government Loan Guarantee Scheme (see below) on which it has consistently charged one of the lowest rates of interest.

Barclays Bank offers an imaginative scheme, the Barclays Business Start Loan discussed in Chapter 3. The purpose is to cover the setting-up costs for new business projects or products for which there is a clear demand. The great advantage of the loans, which can be for up to 100 per cent of the total capital required, from £5,000 to £100,000, is that instead of interest being charged in the usual way the bank charges a royalty based on sales. This means that in the first couple of years' trading, when cash flow problems are likely to be most acute, the repayments will be relatively low. Another advantage is that capital is only repayable at the end of the term, which can be for up to five years. At that stage it would normally be possible to negotiate a more conventional loan. Although the bank will want to see evidence of serious personal financial commitment on the part of the borrowers, it will only expect to take a charge on business assets as security.

Midland Bank offers a Venture Loan Scheme under which small businesses can borrow between £5,000 and £250,000 for up to ten years. Interest is higher than but linked to the Midland base rate and it is sometimes possible to negotiate interest-only payments in the first two years. The bank charges an arrangement fee.

Lloyds Bank offers the Lloyds Enterprise Loan scheme, with loans of between £25,000 and £250,000 repayable over periods of up to ten years. Interest also higher than but linked to the Lloyds base rate is charged, depending on the risks involved. There is not normally any arrangement fee and indeed the bank may be prepared to offer the free services of its business advisory department. In some cases Lloyds may be prepared to lend without security.

National Westminster Bank's main scheme for small businesses is the Business Development Loan. Sums between £2,000 and £250,000 can be borrowed for periods between one and five years. Borrowers are expected to take out life insurance to cover the amount of the loan. Both capital and interest are repayable monthly and the bank charges a handling fee. Unsecured loans may sometimes be made, in which case an extra 1 per cent interest is likely to be charged.

The Government Loan Guarantee Scheme was introduced by the Government in 1981. It is designed to overcome some of the problems faced by new small businesses that have no track record and whose members are unable to provide personal guarantees. All the high street banks as well as some smaller banks and merchant banks participate in the scheme in which the Department of Industry guarantees 80 per cent of every loan, in return for which there is a charge of 3 per cent. The banks, which take 20 per cent of the risk, charge varying rates of interest between 1.5 and 2.5 per cent above base rate. The Co-operative Bank has, as we said earlier, consistently been amongst the most competitive on interest rates on loans advanced under this scheme.

Other financial institutions

Besides the clearing banks there are a number of other possible sources of start-up capital within the financial world. One of these, the Industrial and Commercial Finance Corporation, was described in Chapter 6. It has a great deal of experience of funding small and medium-sized businesses. The chief drawback as far as co-operatives are concerned is that ICFC generally prefers to take a share of the equity of the enterprises in which it invests in return for providing long-term finance at fixed rates of interest. Nevertheless, the Corporation stresses that each application is treated on its merits and a good many loans have been advanced without equity investment on the part of ICFC, so it may well be worth trying.

Another possibility would be to approach a merchant bank or finance house. The latter often provides medium-term loans as well as leasing and hire-purchase arrangements which can be a useful way of easing cash-flow problems in the early years. The subject is dealt with in detail in *Raising Finance: The Guardian Guide For The Small Business* (see above). It is well worth getting hold of a copy of this guide (price £4.95) which includes a much more comprehensive list of addresses than we can give here.

Industrial Common Ownership Finance

ICOF is one of the few organizations set up specifically to finance
worker co-operatives, although since government funding ran
out in 1982 the funds available for lending have been strictly
limited. In the past, ICOF loans have typically been for amounts
between £2,500 and £10,000 repayable over periods up to six
years. At the time of writing, ICOF was discussing with a number
of local authorities the possibility of setting up revolving loan
funds for new co-operatives within their boundaries. In the West
Midlands, for example, £75,000 was made available for lending
on to worker co-ops. So it would be worth checking with your
local CDA or local authority as well as contacting ICOF direct.

Government and local authority finance

Before committing your co-op to the repayment of more or less
expensive loans, make sure that you have exhausted all the
possibilities for raising grants and cheap loans. We have already
mentioned local agencies such as the Department of Industry's
Small Firms Service, Local Enterprise Trusts, local CDAs and, of
course, local authorities themselves which offer help with preparing business plans or finding suitable premises. All should
also be able to advise you about grants or loans for which your
co-operative might be eligible. Some examples of the type of help
available are:

1 In some special development areas, especially where there
  have been coal mine or steel plant closures, new enterprises
  can get low-cost loans and grants to cover the cost of up to 90
  per cent of fixed assets.
2 Capital spending on building small industrial units may be
  eligible for a depreciation allowance of 100 per cent in the first
  year.
3 In Scotland and Wales, the Scottish and Welsh Development
  Agencies provide loan guarantees so that new small businesses
  can borrow from commercial sources.
4 New firms setting up in Inner City Partnership Areas can get
  grants to help with rent and rates, interest-free loans for up to
  two years for site preparation and the installation of services,
  and interest relief grants for loans on land and buildings for

small businesses employing fewer than 50 people.
5 Some local authorities have used their powers under Section 137 of the Local Government Act of 1972 to give grants of up to £1,000 to new worker co-operatives.
6 New businesses setting up in Enterprise Zones are exempt from rates on premises.

New Enterprise Allowance Scheme

An interesting experiment recently introduced by Government is the New Enterprise Allowance Scheme. It was set up in January 1982 in five pilot areas – Coventry, Burnley, the Medway, Kilmarnock and Wrexham – and is designed to encourage unemployed people to set up their own businesses (including co-operatives). You have to be able to invest £1,000 in the enterprise and to have been unemployed for at least 13 weeks to qualify for one allowance of £40 a week for up to a year. The scheme is administered by the Manpower Services Commission and was in 1983 extended to the whole country.

Useful addresses

Co-operative Bank
1 Balloon Street
Manchester M60 4EP
Tel: 061-832 3456

Barclays Bank
Corporate Business Department
Bucklersbury House
3 Queen Victoria Street
London EC4P 4AT
Tel: 01-626 1567

Midland Bank
27-32 Poultry
London EC2P 2BX
Tel: 01-606 9911

Lloyds Bank
71 Lombard Street
London EC3P 3BS
Tel: 01-626 1500
National Westminster Bank
41 Lothbury
London EC2P 2BP
Tel: 01-606 6060
Industrial and Commercial Finance Corporation
91 Waterloo Road
London SE1 8XP
Tel: 01-928 7822
Industrial Common Ownership Finance
4 St Giles Street
Northampton NN1 1AA
Tel: 0604 37563
Manpower Services Commission
Moorfoot
Sheffield S1 4PQ
Tel: 0742 753275

Useful publications

John Pearce, *Sources of Finance for Small Co-operatives* (Industrial Common Ownership Finance)

Barclays Bank, *Two Ways to Build a Business with our Money*

D. S. Watkins, *Raising Finance for the new enterprise – a guide for small firms*, Small Firms Information Centre booklet no. 13 (Department of Industry)

Co-operative Development Agency, *Financial Incentives and Assistance for Industry: A summary of schemes available*

Confederation of British Industry, *Finding Money for your Business*

Industrial and Commercial Finance Corporation, *Borrowing Money for Capital Projects*

National Westminster Bank, *Official Sources of Finance and Aid for Industry in the UK*

London Enterprise Agency, *Sources of Finance for Small Firms Finance for New Projects in the United Kingdom: A guide to government incentives* (Peat, Marwick, Mitchell & Co.)

References

1 Social Democratic Party, *Democracy at work: A policy for part-nership in industry*, Green paper no. 6, 1982
2 Maurice Pearton, *The LSO at 70 – a History of the Orchestra* (Gollancz 1974)
3 G.D.H. Cole, *The Life of Robert Owen* (Macmillan 1925)
4 E.H. Carr, *What is History?* (Cambridge University Trevelyan Lectures 1961; Penguin Books 1981)
5 G.D.H. Cole, *The British Co-operative Movement in a Socialist Society*, a report written for the Fabian Society, London 1951
6 J.D. Chambers, 'The Tawney Tradition', *Economic History Review*, August 1971
7 F. Engels, *The Condition of the Working-Class in England in 1844* (Allen & Unwin 1968)
8 G.N. Ostergaard and A.H. Halsey, *Power in Co-operatives – a Study of the Internal Politics of British Retail Societies* (Blackwell 1965)
9 *Tower Hamlets Co-operator*, April 1888
10 S. and B. Webb, *The Consumers' Co-operative Movement* (Longmans Green 1921)
11 G.D.H. Cole, *A Century of Co-operation* (Co-operative Union, Manchester 1944)
12 E.P. Thompson and E. Yeo, *The Unknown Mayhew* (Merlin Press 1971)
13 S. and B. Webb, *Industrial Democracy* (Longmans Green 1919)
14 Co-operative Development Agency, *Directory of Industrial and Service Co-operatives*, London 1982
15 Robert Oakeshott, *The Case for Workers' Co-ops* (Routledge & Kegan Paul 1978)
16 J. Vanek, *The General Theory of Labor-Managed Market Economies* (Cornell University Press 1970)
17 Peter Jay, *Employment, Inflation and Politics* (Institute of Economic Affairs 1976)

18 James Meade, *Stagflation – Wage Fixing* (Allen & Unwin 1982)

19 K. Coates, 'Democracy and Workers' Control', in J. Vanek (ed.), *Self-Management: Economic Liberation of Man* (Penguin 1975)

20 TEN Co-opérative de Conseils and Mutual Aid Centre, 'Perspectives from West Germany', in *Prospects for Workers' Co-operatives in Europe* (Commission of the European Communities 1981)

21 B. Webb, *The Co-operative Movement in Great Britain* (London 1891; Allen & Unwin 1981)

22 S. and B. Webb, *A Constitution for the Socialist Commonwealth of Great Britain* (Cambridge University Press 1920, reprinted 1975)

23 For example, H. A. Clegg, *A New Approach to Industrial Democracy* (Blackwell 1960)

24 The Webbs when they went to Russia were following a delegation from the Co-operative Union which went in 1929. For this delegation everything was as it should be in the best of all possible worlds. 'In Moscow we did not see any drunken people, and only on one Saturday evening did we see a few cases in Leningrad. Ordinary people expressed contempt for these men, and a notice in the trams requested that they be put on a homeward-bound car.... It was moving in the extreme to stand there and see beneath the working youth of the New Russia, representing with perfect discipline and perfect artistry, scenes from the old regime: long lines of prisoners marching wearily towards Siberian mines; workers staggering under heavy loads with their women helping to bear the yoke; priests invoking the people to submit to authority and power, however corrupt.' *Report of a Group of Co-operators on a visit to Russia* (Co-operative Union August 1929)

25 B. Webb, 'The Discovery of the Consumer', in P. Redfern (ed.), *Self and Society* (Co-operative Wholesale Society 1928)

26 Tony Eccles, *Under New Management* (Pan Books 1981) The story of Britain's largest worker co-operative, its successes and failures

27 As demonstrated in the fullest study yet published, Henk Thomas and Chris Logan, *Mondragon: An Economic Analysis* (Allen & Unwin in conjunction with the Institute of Social Studies at the Hague 1982)

28 Robert Oakeshott, op. cit.; also A. Campbell, C. Keen, G. Norman and R. Oakeshott, *Worker-Owners: The Mondragon Achievement* (Anglo-German Foundation for the Study of Industrial Society 1977)

29 News story in the *Guardian*, 6 October 1982

30 Arnold Bonner, *British Co-operation* (Co-operative Union 1961). Neale and others lost out to 'Baron Wholesale' as he was called by

his enemies, John Mitchell, for long chairman of the cws, whose views are summarized in his own words: 'The three great forces for the improvement of mankind are religion, temperance and Co-operation, and as a commercial force, supported and sustained by the other two, Co-operation is the grandest, noblest and most likely to be successful in the redemption of the industrial classes.'

31 Roger Sawtell and Michael Campbell, *Industrial Co-operatives – A Guide to the ICOM Model Rules* (Industrial Common Ownership Movement, Leeds 1980)

32 Robert Oakeshott, op. cit.

33 Job Ownership Ltd, *Lagun-Aro, the non-profit-making social welfare mutuality of the Mondragon co-operatives* (1982)

34 Labour Party, *Workers Co-operatives*, Discussion Document, 1980

35 B. Webb 'The Discovery of the Consumer', in Redfern (ed.), op. cit.

36 F. Knight, *Risk, uncertainty and profit* (Boston Mass. 1921; republished by London School of Economics and Political Science 1946)

37 'External Finance', Appendix to Job Ownership Limited model rules for a Job Ownership Company

38 Tony Eccles, op. cit.

39 Sir Bernard Miller, Foreword to A. Flanders, R. Pomeranz and J. Woodward, *Experiment in Industrial Democracy: a study of the John Lewis Partnership* (Faber 1968)

40 ibid.

41 Sir George Goyder, *The Future of Private Enterprise, A Study in Responsibility* (Blackwell 1951)

42 Susanna Hoe, *The Man Who Gave His Company Away* (Heinemann 1978)

43 Robert Oakeshott, *Conversions at Mondragon* (Job Ownership Limited 1981)

44 Taken from *In the Making: A Directory of Radical Co-operation* (ITM, 44 Albion Road, Sutton, Surrey 1981)

45 These and others are described in: The Centre for Research on European Women, *New Types of Employment Initiatives Especially as Relating to Women* (The Commission of the European Communities 1981)

46 *Right Livelihood Co-operatives – an Introduction* (Inter-Co-op Secretariat, 51 Roman Road, London E2

47 Arnold Bonner, op. cit.

48 ibid.

49 N. J. Mahoney, 'Promoting Industrial Co-operatives', *Yearbook of*

Agricultural Co-operatives, 1981 (Plunkett Foundation and International Co-operative Alliance)

50 See Robert Oakeshott, *The Case for Workers' Co-ops*, p. 148, table 9.2

51 TEN Co-opérative de Conseils and Mutual Aid Centre, 'Perspectives from Italy', in: *Prospects for Workers' Co-operatives in Europe* (Commission of the European Communities 1981)

52 ibid., 'Perspectives from France'

53 The Norwegian word for co-operative is, literally, 'a many-sided'

54 Henk Thomas and Chris Logan, op. cit.

55 ibid.

56 Chris Logan and Denis Gregory, *Co-operation and Job Creation in Wales: A Feasibility Study* (Wales TUC 1981)

57 The history is recounted by Marianne Rigge, 'Perspectives from Ireland', in: *Prospects for Workers' Co-operatives in Europe* (Commission of the European Communities 1981)

58 From Brent Co-operative Development Agency, Report to the Department of the Environment on progress up to 31 December 1981

59 See R.V.N. Suretts (Executive Secretary of Federation of Agricultural Co-operatives), 'Services for Central Organizations', *Bulletin* 44 (The Society for Co-operative Studies, April 1982)

60 P.R. Dodds and J. Edwards, 'The Central Council and new co-operatives', *Bulletin 44* (The Society for Co-operative Studies, April 1982)

61 Peter Clarke, *Towards Trading Links with Retail Co-operatives* (Co-operative Union 1981)

62 David Owen, *Face the Future* (Jonathan Cape 1981)

63 S.L. Dawson, *Worker Co-operatives and the National Consumer Bank Act* (Industrial Co-operative Association, Cambridge Mass. 1979)

64 See Rodney Clark, *The Japanese Company* (Yale University Press 1979)

65 Cork Committee on Insolvency Law and Practice, HMSO, Cmnd 8558

66 Joan Mitchell, *Proceedings of a National Conference on Management Buyouts – Corporate Trend for the 80s?* (University of Nottingham, Department of Industrial Economics 1981)

67 John Elliott, 'When the employees finance a business', *Financial Times*, 30 October 1981

68 ibid.

69 The Dartington Hall Trust, of which one of the authors is a

member, buys electricity from the grid and distributes it to homes some 800 residents

70 Michael Young, 'Social Work Bolognese', *New Society*, 19 August 1982

71 Mark Goyder, *The Springs of Co-operative Wealth* (Tawney Society, London 1982)

72 Robert Michels, *Political Parties: A Sociological Study of the Oligarchical Tendencies of Modern Democracy* (New York Free Press 1911; reprinted 1958)

73 Adam Smith, *The Wealth of Nations*, vol. 1

74 P. Kropotkin, *Fields, Factories and Workshops Tomorrow*, ed. Colin Ward (Faber 1974)

75 R. Banham, 'Household Godjets', *New Society*, 15 January 1970

76 A. Toffler, *Business Week*, 50th Anniversary Issue, 3 September 1979. Quoted N. Cacace, *Employment and Occupations in Europe in the 1980s* (Council of Europe, Strasbourg 1981)

77 J. Vanek, *The Participatory Economy* (Cornell University Press 1971)

78 C. Clark, *The Conditions of Economic Progress* (Macmillan 1957)

79 V.R. Fuchs, *The Service Economy* (National Bureau of Economic Research, New York 1968)

80 Chris Logan, 'Adapting the Mondragon Experience', unpublished manuscript

81 H.A. Clegg, *Industrial Democracy and Nationalisation*, a study prepared for the Fabian Society, Oxford 1951

82 Chris Logan and Denis Gregory, op. cit.

83 Denis Gregory, *Some lessons from the Workers' Co-ops* (Institute of Workers' Control, Pamphlet no. 80, 1982)

84 John Paul II, *Laborem Exercens*, Encyclical Letter on Human Work (Catholic Truth Society, London 1981)

85 C.A.R. Crosland in writing the Co-operative Independent Commission Report (Co-operative Union 1958) illustrated his belief that successful businesses had to be created if socialism was to fulfil its promise not as the goal but as one of the means towards a fuller life.

Further reading

Antoine Antoni, *The Co-operative Way: Practical advice on self-management in worker co-operatives* (Industrial Common Ownership Movement, Leeds, Pamphlet no. 8, 1979)

Keith Bradley and Alan Gelb, *Industrial Alternatives: Internal Organization and Efficiency in the Mondragon Co-operatives* (London School of Economics and Political Science 1981)

John Cable and Felix FitzRoy, *Co-operation and Productivity: Some evidence from West German Experience* (University of Warwick, Department of Economics, June 1979)

A Call for evidence (Co-operative Party Commission on Employment, July 1981)

Central Council for Agricultural and Horticultural Co-operation, *Annual Reports*

Alastair Campbell, *Worker Ownership* (Industrial Common Ownership Movement 1976)

Paul Chaplin and Roger Cowe, *A survey of contemporary British worker co-operatives* (Manchester Business School 1977)

Peter Clarke, *New Co-operatives – a lightning tour of new literature* (Co-operative Party 1981)

Peter Clarke, *Towards a United Co-operative Movement* (Co-operative Union 1981)

Alasdair Clayre (ed.), *The Political Economy of Co-operation and Participation: A Third Sector* (Oxford University Press 1980)

Peter Cockerton and Rose Bailey, *Co-operative Agency Project: Report of a feasibility study into setting up a local co-operative development agency in the area around Milton Keynes* (Open University 1980)

G.D.H. Cole, *Guild Socialism Restated* (Transaction Books, New Jersey, USA and London 1980)

Community Business Works, A report by a working party set up to consider community self-help groups and local productive activity (Calouste Gulbenkian Foundation, London 1982)

Community Co-operatives – A Guide (Highlands and Islands Development Board 1977)

Community Co-operatives in Rural and Urban Development (Plunkett Foundation, Seventh Co-operative Seminar 1982)

Community self-help: co-operation and mutual aid (Co-operative Documentation Centre Holdings, University of Ulster 1981)

Chris Cornforth, *The Garment Co-operative: an experiment in industrial democracy and business creation* (Co-operatives Research Unit, Open University 1981)

Chris Cornforth, *Trade Unions and producer co-operatives* (Co-operatives Research Unit, Open University 1981)

Co-operative Development Agency, *Annual Reports* from Her Majesty's Stationery Office

Co-operative Research Directory (Co-operatives Research Unit, Open University 1980)

P. Derrick and J. Phipps, *Co-ownership, co-operation and control* (Longmans Green 1969)

Directory of Agricultural, Horticultural and Fishery Co-operatives in the United Kingdom, 1982 (The Plunkett Foundation for Co-operative Studies, Oxford 1982)

Directory of Housing Co-operatives 1981 (The Housing Corporation, April 1981)

The Economics of Worker Co-operatives (Plunkett Foundation, Seventh Co-operative Seminar 1982)

David Ellerman, *Workers' Co-operatives: the Question of Legal Structure*, from Industrial Co-operative Association, 249 Elm Street, Somerville, Mass. 02144, USA

Felix R. FitzRoy, 'Industrial Partnership or Distributional Conflict', unpublished manuscript, August 1979

Royden Harrison, *The Webbs, the Coles and Co-operation* (Co-operative College, Loughborough)

John Spedan Lewis, *Fairer Shares* (Staples Press Ltd, London 1954)

Martin Lockett, *Fakenham Enterprises* (Co-operatives Research Unit, Open University 1978)

David Owen, *Co-operative Ownership* (Industrial Common Ownership Movement and the Co-operative Party 1980)

Rob Paton, *Some problems of co-operative organisation* (Co-operatives Research Unit, Open University 1978)

Rob Paton with Martin Lockett, *Fairblow Dynamics* (Co-operatives Research Unit, The Open University 1978)

John Pearce, *An industrial co-operative experiment in Cumbria* (University of York 1977)

Sidney Pollard, *The Co-operative Ideal – Then and Now* (Co-operative College, Loughborough)

Report of the Working Group on a Co-operative Development Agency (HMSO, Cmnd 6972, October 1977)

Rosemary Rhoades, *Milkwood Co-operative Limited* (Co-operatives Research Unit, Open University 1980)

Samuel Smiles, *Self-Help* (John Murray 1958, centenary edition)

Alan Taylor, *Democratic Planning through Workers' Control* (Socialist Environment and Resources Association (SERA), 9 Poland Street, London W1)

Alan Taylor, *Making the most of workers' co-ops: the local agency approach* (SERA)

Jenny Thornley, *Worker Co-operatives: Jobs and Dreams* (Heinemann Educational Books 1981)

Jenny Thornley, *Workers Co-operatives in France* (Centre for Environment Studies London, Occasional Paper no. 6, 1978)

Jenny Thornley, *The product dilemma for workers' co-operatives in Britain, France and Italy* (Co-operatives Research Unit, Open University 1979)

Eirlys Tynan, Case Studies: *Unit 58, Little Women, Sunderlandia* (Co-operatives Research Unit, Open University 1980)

Jaroslav Vanek (ed.), *Self Management: Economic Liberation of Man* (Penguin Books 1975)

Folkert Wilken, *The Liberation of Capital* (Allen & Unwin 1982)

Michael Young and Marianne Rigge, *Mutual Aid in a Selfish Society* (Mutual Aid Press, 18 Victoria Park Square, London E2 9PF, 1981)

Co-op Development News, prepared by the Network of local CDAs, circulated free to people involved or interested in co-op development work by the Co-operative Union, Holyoake House, Hanover Street, Manchester M60 0AS

Co-operative News, the official journal of the co-operative movement, published weekly, price 9p; Progress House, Chester Road, Manchester M16 9HP

Economic Analysis and Workers' Management, editor Branko Horvat, frequently contains articles on worker co-operatives in a number of different countries. Published quarterly; Smaj Jovina 12, PO Box 611, Belgrade, Yugoslavia

In the Making: A Directory of Radical Co-operation, published annually with occasional supplements; ITM, 44 Albion Road, Sutton, Surrey

Review of International Co-operation, offical journal of the International Co-operative Alliance, published quarterly; ICA, 35 rue des Paquis, POB 41, CH-1211 Geneva, Switzerland

Society for Co-operative Studies Bulletin, editor Dr R.L. Marshall, frequently includes special features on worker co-operatives. Published three times a year; Holly Cottage, 15 Beacon Road, Woodhouse Eaves, Leics LE12 8RN

Index

Aberdeen People's Press, 75
agricultural co-operatives, expansion of, 20, 106–7; importance of, vii, 87; principles of, 42; and support organizations, 105–7
Agriculture Act 1967, 106
Airflow Developments, 72
Alliance, x
alternative movement, attitude to co-operative management, 32; and criticism of modern society, 30–2; middle-class enthusiasm for, 40; as reason for spurt in worker co-operatives, 31–2; and symbol of wholefoods, 7
Amalgamated Union of Engineering Workers, objects of, 143; support for co-ops, 2, 4
Arizmendi, Father, 36, 103
Arts Council, 6
Associazione Generale delle Co-operative Italiane, 83
Avalon Footwear, 1–2

Bader, Ernest, 71–2, 77
Bader, Godric, 72
Bank for Co-operative Development, 112–28
Barclays Bank, address, 169; Business Start Loan, 59, 124, 166; royalties, 59
Barclays Merchant Bank, 126
Basque country, tradition of saving in, 52
Beecham, Sir Thomas, 5

Beechwood College, 101–2, 161–2; address of, 163
Benthamite utilitarianism, 14–15
Bewley's Cafes, 72
Blanc, Louis, 84
bonus shares, need for tax concession in issue of, 107
bonuses, for work invested, 46
Bourlet Frames, 72–3
Brent Co-operative Development Agency, 93–4
Bristol Musicals Co-operative, 75
Bristol Printers, 46
British Technology Group, 116–17
Buddhism, 77
building societies, 18
Burke, Edmund, 149
business plan, 157–9

Caja Laboral Popular, attitude to conversions, 73–4; Empresarial Division of, 37; firmness of management by, 37; information possessed by, 111; maximum size of co-ops allowed by, 137; as supplier of capital, 37, 85; support for co-ops from, 85; training of managers by, 37; see also Mondragon
Cambridge Co-operative, 116
Campbell, Cairns, 92
Campbell, Mike, 88
Campbell, Ronald, 11–12
capital, advantage of conversions, 78; equity, 49; external, 56–60;

capital—*cont.*
loan, 50; personal stakes, 48;
shortage of, 49, 56–60
capitalist attitudes in worker co-ops,
50
capitalist system, ix; challenge of co-
ops to, 21; moral underpinning
for, 15
Central Council for Agricultural and
Horticultural Co-operation, 81,
106
Christian Socialists, 30, 40, 79
Clark, Colin, 137
class struggle in industry, 23, 30, 140
closed shop in co-ops, 4, 6
Coates, Ken, 29
collectivist versus individualist
debate, 48–56
community co-operatives, 8
companies, class struggle in, 23; as
collective enterprise, 22;
management accountability in, 23
Companies Acts, 88, 154
company form, advantages of, 107–8
company management, criticism of,
viii–ix, 23–4, 143, 146–7
competition, as moral underpinning
of capitalism, 14–15; paradox of
need for in co-operatives, 27–8
Confederation of British Industry, 98
Confédération Générale des SCOP, 43
Confederazione Co-operative
Italiane, 82
Conseil Supérieur de la Co-opération,
85
consortia, in Italian co-operatives, 83
consultancy, the need for, 111–12
consumer co-operatives, *see* retail
societies
control, viii; by all members, 44;
outsider, 45
conversions, advantage of company
form in, 107; advantages of, 78;
attitude of Mondragon to, 73–4;
role of new bank in, 118–19; *see
also* John Lewis Partnership,

National Freight Corporation,
Scott Bader Commonwealth
co-operation between co-operatives,
47–8
Co-operative Bank, address, 169; as
candidate for new bank, 116; as
current account holder of worker
co-ops, 112; establishment of, 81;
participation in Government Loan
Guarantee Scheme, 165–6; special
scheme for worker co-ops, 165–6
Co-operative College, 87
co-operative companies, investment
by government in, 127
Co-operative Companies Act, 108
Co-operative Congress, 89
Co-operative Development Agency,
20; address, 156; as candidate for
new bank, 116, 118; dealings with
government, 90; as federal body,
98; history of, 89–91; membership
of, 44; model rules, 154–5;
registration of co-ops, 154;
relationship with ICOM, 99; as
support organization, 43
Co-operative Insurance Society, 81
co-operative management,
accountability to members of, 44;
appointment of, 44; *see also*
weaknesses of co-operatives
Co-operative Party, 93; alliance with
Labour Party, 38–40; and self-help
movement, 38
Co-operative Productive Federation,
43; history and merger with Co-
operative Union, 87–8
Co-operative Productive Federation
societies, 74; distribution of assets
by, 46; membership of, 44; outside
shareholders in, 45
Co-operative Retail Services, 2, 57;
establishment of, 81; as outside
shareholders in CPF societies, 47
Co-operative Union, establishment
of, 81; links with Labour Party,
87; as support organization, 42–3

Co-operative Wholesale Society, 2; and community co-operatives, 9; establishment of, 81
Cork Committee, 122
Craigton Bakery, 62, 67–8
Crédit Agricole, 84–5
credit unions, principles of, 42

Danish experience, 145
Darwin, Charles, 14
decision-making, collective, 7; by entire workforce, 67; by members, 3; by whole board, 5
demarcations, disappearance of, 4, 63
democracy, pluralist view of, 33; survival of, 26
Department of Industry Small Firms Service, 158–9, 164, 168
discrimination against co-operatives, 109–11
distribution of assets on winding up, 46
distribution of profits, as bonuses, 46; danger of capital depletion by, 50–1
division of labour, 131–3, 138–9
division of two sides of industry, 23
Dunlop Company, 2–4

Eccles, Tony, 35, 102
Ecology Party, 93
education, 17; as fifth principle, 47
election of directors, 44
Electrical, Telecommunications and Plumbing Union, 143
Emilia Romagna, co-ops in, 83
Employment Protection Act, 120
Engels, Friedrich, 15–16
Enterprise Allowances, 109
Eriskay community co-operative, 8–12
European Economic Community, 144
Evans, Moss, 145
expansion, 55

family, informal co-operative of the, 133–5, 137; as model of co-operation, 148–9
federation, freedom to attack government, 113; need for, 96–9
Federation of Agricultural Co-operatives, 106
Federation of Northern Wholefood Co-ops, 8
Federation of Radical Booksellers, 75
finance, government, 114; how to raise, 165–70; need for new bank, 112
Finance Act, 1978, 90, 107, 127
Finance for Industry Group, 117
Fourier, Charles, 84
France, co-operative experience in, 83–5; tax advantages of co-ops in, 108–9
Friends of the Western Buddhist Order, 77

Government Small Business Loan Guarantee Scheme, 167
government support, for agricultural co-operatives, 106; capital needed, 128; encouragement of conversions, 78; finance for co-operatives, 114
Goyder, George, 72
Grand National Consolidated Trades Union, 14
Grand National Moral Union of the Productive Classes, 14, 41
Greater London Enterprise Board, 158–9
Gregory, Denis, 145–6
Groupement National de la Co-operation, 84–5
guarantee companies, disadvantages of, 107
Guardian Guide for the Small Business, 167
Guild Socialism, 18, 30; in modern form, 41

Guild Socialists, 18, 40, 79; and trade union management, 18

Health and Safety at Work Act, 145-6
Highlands and Islands Development Board, 8, 92, 114
housing co-operatives, vii, 20; and CDA Working Group minority report, 90; principles of, 42

Inchinnan Engineering Limited, 2-4, 62, 64, 78
incomes policies, 25
individualist versus collectivist debate, 48-56
Industrial and Commercial Finance Corporation, address of, 170; as candidate for new bank, 116-18; funding for co-ops, 167; in management buy-outs, 123-6
Industrial Common Ownership Act, 1976, 71; appointment of official bodies under, 91; passage of, 88
Industrial Common Ownership Finance, 94, 168; address of, 170; as candidate for new bank, 116; establishment of, 88
Industrial Common Ownership Movement, 20; address of, 156; as federal body, 98; membership of, 44; relationship with CDA, 99; as support organization, 43, 44, 88-9
Industrial Common Ownership Movement co-operatives, distribution of assets in, 47; model rules of, 51, 88, 153-4; nominal shareholding in, 51; registration of, 154; shortage of capital in, 58
Industrial and Provident Societies Acts, 42, 88; disadvantages of, 107
Industrial Revolution, 22; cotton masters in the, 13-14; separation of work and leisure by, 148
industrialization, effects of, 148-9
industry, bitterness in, viii

inflation, viii; and effects on capital stakes, 49; and the unions, 24; and wages, 26
Inner City Partnership Area grants, 168
Inner Urban Areas Act, 1972, 95
inter-co-operative support, 83
interest, fixed, 50; limited, 45-6; loan, 46
International Co-operative Alliance, 42-8, 80
Italy, experience of co-ops, 82-3; number of co-ops, 20; social work co-ops, 126; trade unions, 145

Japanese banks, 111, 114
Japanese co-operative experience, 114-16
Jay, Peter, 26
Job Ownership Limited, 43, 91; address of, 156; in individualist versus collectivist debate, 51-2; influence of Mondragon on, 51
Job Ownership Limited co-ops, capital contributions to, 52; constitution of, 53; distribution of assets in, 47; membership of, 44; registration of, 155; treatment of inflation by, 52
John Lewis Partnership, 20, 69-71
Jones, George, 91

Kennington Office Cleaners Co-operative, 76-7, 78
Keynes, Maynard, 58
Kirkby Manufacturing and Engineering, 35, 62
Knight, Frank, 58
Kropotkin, Peter, 61, 132

Labour Government Working Group, 89-90
labour only co-ops, 82
Labour Party, attitude to House of Lords, 142; attitude to Mondragon, 54; call for Co-

operative Development Agency,
89; Clause 4, 29; formation of, 19;
links with co-operative movement,
87; in self-help movement, 38;
Working Group, 1980, 54
Lawrence, Dennis, 91
Lebensreform, 102
Lega Nazionale delle Co-operative e
Mutue, 82-3
legislation, proposal for new, 108
Lenin (Vladimir Ilich Ulianov), 23
Lewis, John Spedan, 69
Liberal Party, 19
Lloyds Bank, address of, 170;
Enterprise Loan Scheme, 166
loan capital, effect on gearing of, 57
local authorities, attraction of co-ops
to, 110-11; support for local co-
operative development agencies,
93-5
local co-operative development
agencies, 93-5; directory of, 155
Local Enterprise Development Unit,
158-9
Local Government Act, 1972,
Section 137, 169
London Co-operative Society, 57
London Philharmonic Orchestra, 4-
7
London Symphony Orchestra, 4

MacInnes, Iain, 9-11
MacMillan, Father J.A., 11
management, absence of, 7;
accountability of, ix, 22-4, 142-3;
attitudes of, 146-7; in a
community co-operative, 9;
control by, viii; in conversions, 78;
lack of, 8; in nationalized
industries, 28-9; need for, 44; need
for improvement in, 99-103;
power of, viii, 28-9
Manchester Cold Rollers, 74-5
Manpower Services Commission,
169; New Enterprise Allowance
Scheme, 169

Manuest, 84
Marx, Karl, and class struggle, 23;
and division of labour, 131, 133
Mayhew, Henry, 19-20
Meade, James, 26-8
mechanization, effects on jobs,
135
Meidner Plan, 127
membership of co-operatives,
outsider, 44-5; restricted to
workers, 44; voluntary and open,
43-4
Metro Books Co-operative, 75
Michels, Robert, 131, 140
middle class, co-operatives, 4, 30;
enthusiasm for worker co-ops, 40
Midland Bank, address of, 169;
Venture Loan Scheme, 166
Miller, Sir Bernard, 70
Mitchell, Professor Joan, 124
Mitsubishi, 115
Mondragon co-operatives, attitude
to conversions, 73-4; bonuses in,
49; capital accounts in, 53; capital
depletion in, 53; collective versus
individualist shareholding in, 52;
discipline over, 114; education in,
36, 86; employment in, 36;
Empresarial Division of, 128;
example of, 35-8; General
Assembly of, 38; ICOM attitude to,
98; quality of managers in, 37, 40;
research and development in, 86;
research on, 102; social security in,
86; steady expansion of, 36;
support system of, 85-6; trade
groupings in, 85-6; wages in, 25,
36; and Wales TUC, 144; worker
investment in, 37
monetarism, 24-5
monopolies, danger of, 27
Monopolies Commission, 27
Morley, John, 106
Musicians' Union, 6
mutual friendly societies, 18
mutual insurance societies, 18

National Building Guild, 18
National Consumer Co-operative Bank, 112
National Extension College, 102, 161-2
National Federation of Credit Unions, 90
National Freight Corporation, 69, 125-6
National Westminster Bank, address of, 170; Business Development Loan, 166
nationalization, attitude of trade unionists to, 41; failure of, 28-30, 40, 41
nationalized industries, 23; accountability in, 28; state control of, viii
Neale, E.V., 42
neighbourhood service co-operatives, 90
New Enterprise Allowance Scheme, 169
New Enterprise Programme Centres, 162
New Lanark, 13
new start co-operatives, 74-7
Northumbrian Energy Workshop, 75

Oakeshott, Robert, 23, 36, 40
Open University, 102
origins of co-operatives, 61-78; see also conversions, new start co-operatives, rescues
Otley Woodwind Co-operative, 75
Owen, David, 109
Owen, Robert, 13-14, 15, 20, 40, 61, 79, 100
Owenism, 14
Owenites, 13-15
ownership, vii, viii, ix, 22-3

Philharmonia, 4
Plunkett Foundation for Co-operative Studies, 103, 106
Pope John Paul II, 148

Potter, Beatrice, see Webb
premises, where to get help finding, 164-5
principles of co-operation, 42
private ownership, 22-3
private sector, vii
productive co-operative societies, distribution of assets in, 46; growth and decline of, 18; take-over by outsiders of, 45
Psychological Therapy Service, 75
public ownership, 18

Randolph Leisurewear, 68-9
redundancy payments, investment of, 3
Registrar of Companies, address of, 156; role in conversions, 119
Registrar of Friendly Societies, 42-3, 88, 107, 153; address of, 156
rescues, 61-9; case for, 123-4; need for advice in, 78; need for support organizations, 63; role of new bank, 119-22; role of shop stewards, 62; see also Craigton Bakery, Inchinnan Engineering, Toptown Printers
research, need for, 102-3
retail co-operative societies, vii, 17-18, 20; dominance of, 18; in formation of CDA, 89; in membership of worker co-operatives, 44; principles of, 42; shortage of capital in, 33-4, 56-7; and sixth principle, 80; struggle to hold share of market, 20
Right Livelihood Co-operatives, 77
risk factor, 58
Rochdale Co-operative Building Society, 81
Rochdale Co-operative Card Manufacturing Society, 81
Rochdale Co-operative Insurance Society, 81
Rochdale Co-operative Manufacturing Society, 45

Rochdale Equitable Provident Sickness and Burial Society, 81
Rochdale Equitable Society, 80
Rochdale Pioneers, 7, 15–18, 45, 80–1
Royal Arsenal Co-operative Society, 93
Royal Philharmonic Orchestra, 4

Scott Bader Commonwealth, 21, 71–2; support for ICOF, 88; support for other co-operatives, 78
Scottish Co-operative Development Committee, 3, 67–8; model rules and registration, 155; as support organization, 91–2
Scottish Development Agency, funding for co-operatives, 92, 158, 159, 168
Scottish Trades Union Congress, 144
self-employment, vii
self-government, 15
self-interest, 14–16
self-management, vii
service co-operatives, 21, 83, 126
services, rise in numbers engaged in, 137–8
share capital, 50; advantages of, 58; in community co-operatives, 9
shares, equity, 58; non-voting preference, 59; right to buy, 4
Shoko Chukin Bank, 115
Smith, Adam, 15, 131–2
Smith doctrine, 15, 34
Social Democratic Party, x
Sociétés Co-opératives Ouvrières de Production (SCOP), 43; support for, 84
Soviet communism, Webbs' view of, 33
Soviet Union, nationalization in, 30
Spare Rib, 75
stagflation, 24–8
state, role of, 104–28; support for agricultural co-operatives, 105–7
state ownership, 29

state sector, vii
state socialism, 18, 21, 28
state support, in Italy, 83
SUMA, 7–8, 99

Taunton Shirt Co-operative, 41
Tawney, R.H., 15
Technical Development Capital Ltd., 117
technological change, advantages of, 135–7
Thatcher Government, increase in unemployment under, 142; policy on unemployment, 24–5; and Smith doctrine, 15
third sector, vii
Thomas, Henk and Logan, Chris, 85
Thompson, Peter, 125–6
time-keeping in co-operatives, 3
Toffler, Alvin, 136
tolerance, need for, 60; as seventh principle, 55
Toptown Printers, 62, 64–7, 69, 101
trade unions, attitudes, x; to co-operatives, 141–6; to management, 141; of members, 131; to workers' control, 38
trade unions, accountability of leaders, 142–3; anti-capitalist stance of, 19; closed shops, 6; demarcations in, 4; expressions of solidarity by, 20; formation of, 19; in labour trinity, 38; and nationalization, 143; as permanent opposition, 144; in productive co-ops, 2; role of opposition in industry, 41; sponsored co-ops, 41; struggle for recognition by, 19
Trades Union Congress, 98
training, need for, 101–3; where to get help, 160–3
Transport and General Workers' Union, 41, 143, 144–5

Ulgor, 85–6
unemployment, in Britain, 24; need for new initiatives to solve, 128

unity, need for, 55
unpaid work, satisfaction of, 140;
    trade-off with paid work, 129

Vienna Congress of the International
    Co-operative Alliance, 46
voluntary membership, 43–4
voting, 44–5

wage-cost-price spiral, 26
wage levels, 4, 7, 25–7
wages, fund, 127; pressure for
    increase in, 24; in rescues, 63
Wales Co-operative Development
    Centre, 144
Wales Trades Union Congress, as
    co-operative support organization,
    92; new initiative by, 144–5
Wandsworth Enterprise
    Development Agency, 94
weaknesses of co-operatives, low
    calibre of management, 34, 79–80,
    99–103; shortage of capital, 33–4,
    56, 59, 79–80
Webb, Beatrice and Sidney, and
    Guild Socialism, 33; and the

Labour Party Constitution, 29–30;
    their opposition to worker co-
    operatives, x, 33–4, 40, 56, 59, 79,
    100–1, 150; and trade unions, 20,
    33, 35
Wedgwood Benn co-operatives, 34–
    5, 109
Welsh Development Agency, 158–9,
    168
West Germany, 32, 102, 110
Wigston Hosiers, 47
women's co-operatives, 75–7
Woolf, Ralph, 91
worker co-operatives, building and
    industrial, 21; definition of, vii–
    viii, 42; growth of, 1, 20–2;
    investment in, 3; labour intensive,
    21; in services, 21, 83, 126
workers' buy-outs, 121, 123–7
workers' control, in Clause 4, 29–30;
    in modern form, 41, 144
workers, as employers, 25; as inside
    shareholders, ix
Writers and Readers Publishing Co-
    operative, 75

Yugoslavia, 49